MINERAL
KINGDOM
WISDOM ™

Crystal Deva Cards™

THE MINERAL KINGDOM'S MESSAGES OF HOPE & SELF-EMPOWERMENT FOR THE NEW MILLENNIUM

PRESENTED THROUGH
CINDY WATLINGTON
Photographs By Rick Kopp

INNER QUEST
PUBLISHING
BOX 17234 BOULDER, COLORADO 80308

Dedicated

To the evolution of a new consciousness through self-discovery and personal transformation.

To the reawakening of the sacred partnership of mutual support, love, and cooperation among all the Kingdoms.

To the healing of Mother Earth and Her family through compassion, tolerance, and generosity.

Table Of Contents

From The Author

About The Crystal Deva Cards

Using The Crystal Deva Cards

The Messages Of
The Crystal Devas

From
The
Author

In Appreciation

*THE CRYSTAL DEVA CARDS WOULD NOT HAVE BEEN
POSSIBLE WITHOUT THE LOVE AND SUPPORT OF MANY DEAR
FRIENDS. I WILL ALWAYS BE GRATEFUL FOR THEIR HELP.*

To the Mineral Kingdom, for selecting me to be your representative for this project and for trusting me with the awesome responsibility of translating your concepts into the written word. I am honored. Thank you for your continued friendship, guidance, strength, and balance.

To my soulmate, best friend, and husband, Rick Kopp, for your unswerving belief in me and my work. Your love and synergistic support throughout our life together has been an incredible blessing. Thank you for lending your special talents of photography, art direction and production, advertising, and marketing to this endeavor—without which it could not have happened. I am so happy to share my life with you..

To my special friend, Gwilda Miller, for shepherding me through the deep, dark, scary places to help me face the goblins there. I respect so much the rightmindedness you bring to your work and the example you set for courage. Thank you, in addition, for unselfishly sharing your mineral friends to help complete the *Crystal Deva Cards* family.

To my dear "sister and brother," Katie and Gregory Riddael, for the sincere friendship, integrity, and support you have offered throughout our relationship and for this undertaking. Thank you for blessing this work with your energy and for the generous contribution of your stone allies to the *Crystal Deva Cards*.

To my friends, helpers, and guides, on all the Planes, who have been advocates of my growth and well-being. Thank you for offering your love, encouragement, and healing so that I could help make the *Crystal Deva Cards* a reality.

11

The Author's
Evolution and Purpose

HOW DID I COME TO BE PART OF THE
CRYSTAL DEVA CARDS PROJECT?
HOW DID I GET FROM WHERE I'VE BEEN
TO WHERE I AM TODAY?

TWENTY YEARS FROM BELIEF TO ACTION. After a rewarding career in Special Education as a classroom teacher and administrator, I entered the business world and became a marketing manager with a Fortune 100 company.

At first, it was exciting. But after a while, the generous salary, benefits, and prestige of a corporate life felt empty and meaningless. Each day, there was less of me present. I knew, intuitively, that if I didn't create a life for myself that centered around the spiritual and the creative, my soul would begin to shrivel and die.

In the Seventies, I had been exposed to metaphysical principles. As a result of these teachings, I changed. I saw things differently.

13

Although the material world still captured much of my attention, I always came back for more esoteric study. These classes and books made me feel as though I had found my true home.

Once again, I began to remember and live what I had learned from these metaphysical teachings. I came to trust that if I listened to my heart, it would guide me to my true purpose. Who would have guessed that it would take twenty years for me to act on that belief. Finally, with real faith, I left my corporate job. Half the people I knew thought I was crazy; the other half were envious.

THE STONES SPEAK. Freedom from the fast track opened a space in me that allowed a connection to the world of crystals and the Mineral Kingdom. After training in the art of gold and silversmithing, I began to create jewelry using crystals in their natural state, uncut and unpolished. When people would ask, "How do you know how to set the stones?" I would answer, "The crystals tell me what they want." And they did. My goal was to have others experience the esoteric wisdom and healing properties that the stones offered. I hoped to be a Johnny Appleseed for the Mineral Kingdom.

The business grew and prospered. My husband, who had been a corporate advertising director, left his job to take over the jewelry business' marketing, advertising, and public relations. But once again, I found myself replicating an old pattern. I was allowing my outer life to dominate and interfere with my inner life. I rarely made time to communicate with the Mineral Kingdom. I was in "Type A" behavior mode again and caught in the same trap that I had escaped from only a few years before. It turned out that we didn't own the business, it owned us.

THE DARK NIGHT OF THE SOUL. After five very intense and successful years, we both felt that our lives needed to change radically. We moved to a different part of the country to take some much needed "time off for good behavior." We renovated a vintage log lodge in the mountains outside Boulder, Colorado and wrote a book. Then, we had a life-altering automobile accident.

While rehabilitating over the next several years, I experienced the dark night of the soul—that place of confusion, desperation, and despair that leaves you hopeless and floundering. During this time, I reevaluated every aspect of my life. Who am I? Why am I here? What am I meant to do with my life?

It was after much soul-searching, meditation, and prayer that one day I spoke to the Universe and said, "If You have special work for me to do, I need specific information about what it is. I'm waiting for your guidance."

THE STONES SPEAK AGAIN. Later that same day, hiking in the foothills of Boulder, my attention was sharply drawn to a small rock ten feet or so off the path. As I picked it up, I could clearly see the impression of an angel etched in its surface. Moments later, the words "Crystal Deva Cards" came into my mind.

I knew immediately that I was, once again, to be a vehicle for the Mineral Kingdom—this time to present their words of inspiration and illumination as a gift of love to the Human Kingdom. Here was the guidance I had been longing to hear for so long. Without hesitation or doubt, I joyfully accepted my assignment. It has been a great honor to have participated in helping them speak to all of us.

A SHIFT IN CONSCIOUSNESS. This is a special time in history. Those of us who are here now have chosen to be present for a shift in consciousness that Planet Earth has never before experienced. It is a time of accelerated growth, clarity, and self-discovery. Most of what we have known is beginning to change. Once again, we will remember our partnership with the other Kingdoms and communicate with them for our mutual education and support. Through the opening of our hearts and our psyches, we will heal ourselves and Mother Earth.

Most of us recognize the divisiveness in our world. To create peace and harmony, we must move from our obstinately-held belief systems and isolated, self-contained camps to a new position of openness, flexibility, and peace-making. If each of us can create a bridge of understanding, compromise, and respect between factions at opposite ends of the continuum, there will be no wars, discrimination, or separatism.

A BRIDGE. It's my desire to serve as a bridge of Light, Love, and Communication. I offer myself as a voice to those in the other Kingdoms and the unseen realms—who have a language that most of us, as yet, do not understand. I hope to be a peacemaker among those polarized by superstition and fear over differences in belief systems, color, ethnicity, or sexual preference. I want to alleviate the hopelessness of humankind by introducing people to the Universe's love and support.

My heart spoke so loudly and insistently that I had to offer what I could to make a difference. There was no denying its persistent persuasion. I encourage you to search your heart and ask the Universe what you can do to make our world happier and healthier. A bonus that I didn't expect when I started working on this project was the immense joy I would feel. I wish the same experience for you. All of us have something special to give.

IT's UP TO EACH OF US. Let's make Peace more personal. World peace seems so huge and unattainable. We must start individually if we expect changes globally. Each day, in every interaction we have, let's try to really listen to the other person and respond from a place of non-judgment and love. If we wait around for world leaders to bring about Peace, it will never happen. It's up to each of us to make our world the beautiful place it's meant to be.

About The
Crystal
Deva Cards

The Purpose Of The Crystal Deva Cards

LONG AGO, A SACRED PACT WAS MADE.
ALL THE KINGDOMS—HUMAN, ANIMAL, PLANT AND
MINERAL—PLEDGED TO SUPPORT EACH OTHER.
NOW, AS THE NEW MILLENNIUM APPROACHES,
THE STONES SENSE OUR TURMOIL AND OFFER THEIR FRIENDSHIP.
THEY SPEAK TO HELP US REMEMBER WHAT WE ONCE KNEW,
BUT FORGOT...OUR ABILITY TO CREATE A FULFILLING AND
MEANINGFUL LIFE.

WHO ARE THE CRYSTAL DEVAS? They are Beings of Light, special emissaries of the Mineral Kingdom, guardians and overseers of the individual stones.

Collectively, they are under the stewardship of their mentor, the Overlighting Deva of the Mineral Kingdom. The Overlighting Deva watches over the well-being of all mineral entities, including mountains, volcanoes, and Mother Earth Herself.

WHY DO THE CRYSTAL DEVAS WANT TO COMMUNICATE WITH US? As our planetary sisters and brothers, they feel much affection for us. Since the first humans walked the planet, the Mineral Kingdom has watched our progress here. In ancient times, they observed our power to create happiness and abundance for ourselves and Mother Earth. Because we lived according to Universal Principles, our lives were full of confidence and free of fear. Tragically, over the millennia, we forgot our birthright of self-empowerment, and hope faded from our lives.

Now, the Crystal Devas speak, to help us remember how to reclaim our power and transform our lives. They step forward in this card deck and book to bring messages of self-empowerment and hope for all of humanity. They offer an evolution of consciousness and an escape from the entrapment of emotional entanglements.

The Crystal Devas sense the chaos and anguish of our existence. Their comforting messages soften the blow of these turbulent times and let us know that we are not alone. In the *Crystal Deva Cards*, they lovingly accompany and support us through an exploration of ourselves and the human condition. Allow them to guide you to a new awareness of your talents and attributes, help you overcome your challenges, and realize your potential.

WE HAVE A NEW LIFE AHEAD OF US. The New Millennium holds the potential for an entirely different existence for Planet Earth and all its family. The space/time continuum is opening to release the old and accept the new.

Like no other time in history, change will affect every aspect of our lives and our world. It has been prophesied for thousands of years that this would be the time of the Great Awakening. You may feel as though you have aroused from a long night's sleep to find yourself in another place and time. You will, in actuality, step from one reality to another, from the dark into the light. In the process, you will shed layer upon layer of excess baggage you have been carrying.

This is also a time when old, inaccurate belief systems are crumbling and giving way to the Truth. Our vision has been blurred by our world's emotional traumas and dramas. At last, we see more clearly. We realize that influences, on the planet and beyond, have used us as puppets in their own manipulative theatrical production. Now that we realize what's been going on, we can take back control of our lives. Collectively, we are beginning to shift our focus from fear, uncertainty, hatred, and separatism to faith, confidence, love, and cooperation.

MINERAL KINGDOM'S MISSION. The *Crystal Deva Cards* are an outgrowth of the Mineral Kingdom's mission: to ease our emotional and spiritual suffering; to help us rediscover and reclaim our inherent power; and to reestablish communication and cooperation among all the Kingdoms—Human, Animal, Plant, and Mineral.

The Crystal Devas remind us that all living entities are part of the same family. All lifeforms everywhere are composed of the same Universal Essence. There is no separation, even though our appearances would make us think otherwise. Differences in physical composition are designed as a test to determine if we can see beyond the less significant exterior to the more important interior.

BEHIND THE MASK. The other Kingdoms recognize who we really are behind our masks. Once we recognize the Universal Essence within each of them, we have the potential for a new partnership built on respect, caring, and teamwork. Together, we can once again restore Mother Earth to a state of harmony, health, and peace.

The Interconnectedness Of All Creatures

AT THE BEGINNING OF PLANET EARTH'S HISTORY, THE CREATOR ARCHITECT DEVISED A MASTER PLAN FOR THE WELL-BEING OF ALL.

Every member of the Animal, Plant, Mineral, and Human Kingdoms was stationed here to complete a unique mission. Each had a special role to play. No creature could replace the work of another. The life of every being was sacred and critical.

All entities were equal, inter-dependent, mutually responsible, living in cooperative harmony and respect. There was no separation, no division, no hierarchy of superior and inferior. Each Kingdom relied on the others for support as it pursued its often challenging assignments.

WE ARE THE CARETAKERS. Our Creator's intention was to entrust the Human Kingdom with the special assignment of Caretaker of the Earth and its inhabitants. In the beginning, we understood our mission and treated all life with love and respect. But as the centuries passed, we moved farther away from our blessed existence in Nature, and we forgot our roles as guardians. We began to treat other lifeforms differently.

Some humans began to see themselves as superior to other beings. When the Bible said that humans should have dominion over the Earth, they translated *dominion* to mean *domination.* They interpreted these Holy words as proof of their God-given superiority. They assumed that this "superiority" gave them license to do whatever they wanted, as a right.

Many concluded that the lives of other entities were less valuable and therefore, expendable. Other lifeforms had significance only so far as they provided profit or pleasure for Humans. For the "Greater Good," we wiped out animal species through hunting, eliminated old-growth forests through clear cutting, and ravaged the Earth through mining. Instead of taking the Earth's inhabitants under our wing, we've held them under our thumb.

Most of us may never personally destroy with gun, saw, or shovel. But through indifference, we can become co-conspirators in the extinction of members of our fellow Kingdoms. It was intended that we be their guardians, but, unintentionally, we have betrayed them. When a species is eradicated, the spiritual mission entrusted to them is never completed and the benefit is lost to us all.

How has our species become so insensitive and unresponsive to the welfare of our kinsfolk? These fellow animals, plants and minerals are our family. We are not their superiors; we are all equals. If we dismiss any other entity as insignificant, we disrupt the Divine Plan and tamper with our own fate. Until we raise our consciousness to recognize that every being has purpose and value, we are not humane—we are merely human.

WORKING COOPERATIVELY. If we are to save our Earth and ourselves—all living beings must work together. We must develop a relationship with our planetary brothers and sisters that is worthy of their trust. But is this possible?

After the thoughtless and cruel treatment they've been subjected to, will the other Kingdoms want anything to do with us? If someone had treated us in the same way, could we forgive and forget?

Fortunately, the other Kingdoms see the bigger, more important issue—the common good of all. They have not forgotten our ancient alliance of collaboration and mutual support. To help us remember and reinstate the old ways, they offer forgiveness and friendship.

Our first step toward re-establishing our sacred fellowship with the other Kingdoms is to honor the presence of every other being as our equal. We can demonstrate this respect by staying conscious and being responsible, by preserving and not poisoning the Earth, and by being a friend.

The next step is to establish communication. You may think that our respective languages are far too different for us to ever truly connect. In reality, since we are all composed of the very same essence, there is a Universal language available to make conversation possible.

NOW IS THE TIME. The members of the other Kingdoms are eager to speak with us. Ordinarily, they would wait patiently in hopes that an opportunity for contact might occur when we slow down, quiet our minds, and become receptive. However, the challenges of our planetary crisis have motivated the other Kingdoms to reach out to us more insistently. Our world is sick and polluted. Our ecosystems are shutting down. Planet Earth needs our help.

Our friends in the other Kingdoms want to help us as well as the planet. They feel our pain and distress. We need the support and companionship of the other Kingdoms for our emotional, physical, and spiritual stability. They have much to teach us and we have much to learn. Our segregation from each other has robbed us of a valuable support system. We all need each other if we hope to survive.

Now is the time for reconciliation, reintegration, and reunion. There can be no excuses or procrastination. Let's make the time NOW—before it runs out.

Introduction To The Mineral Kingdom

MINERALS HAVE MORE IMPACT ON OUR LIVES THAN ANY OTHER KINGDOM. WHERE WOULD WE BE WITHOUT THEM? SINCE THE EARTH ITSELF IS A ROCK, WE'D BE WITHOUT OUR FOUNDATION.

Minerals create materials and machinery used in transportation, agriculture, manufacturing, communication, and health care. Whether it's the fertile soil of a farm, your computer, or a vitamin tablet, minerals make an important contribution to our lives.

Beyond the obvious, minerals have other qualities which influence us. The Ancients were convinced that the vibrations of treasured gemstones made a positive impression on their lives. They wore these stones in crowns and breastplates for their power as much as for their beauty. Throughout the millennia, we have continued to adorn ourselves with jewelry, perhaps sensing a mystical connection. In the last thirty years or so, there has been a resurgence of interest in crystals and stones for their metaphysical properties.

BALANCE AND HARMONY. Today, it's commonly accepted in scientific circles that quartz crystals are amplifiers of energy. They are used in the electronics, time-keeping, and communication industries. The same energy that makes them such a valuable tool in science also affects the body's electromagnetic field for balancing and healing. All minerals have vibrational properties that are helpful to human stability and health.

One of the greatest challenges we humans have, is dealing with our emotions. We are besieged by emotional turmoil—addiction, depression, questions of purpose, problems of self-confidence and self-esteem, concerns over identity, and issues of control and power.

The Earth is a metaphor for the human emotional condition. If you've ever experienced a natural disaster—an earthquake, a flood, an avalanche, or volcano—you're immediately shocked into consciousness that the earth's stable appearance is deceiving. Its solid outer body hides a core of bubbling molten rock. Similarly, our outward appearance may fool others as well. We may look cool and steady on the surface, while inside we're ready to explode or fall apart.

As humans, we experience our own natural disasters—anger, fear, jealousy, grief, love. Intense emotional episodes or difficult life situations can leave us struggling for stability and lead to physical illness.

MINERALS AND HUMANS. Many health practitioners and metaphysicians believe that a malady in the physical body originates in the lighter, etheric bodies that surround us and are invisible to the physical eyes. The cause of a physical illness may be an emotional or spiritual issue from this or a past lifetime that needs to be confronted, completed, and released.

Crystals and all minerals offer a faithful and compassionate service to humans in the balancing of the emotional and spiritual bodies. They offer us their counsel and friendship. The application of crystals to the chakra areas helps many regain their health and composure. Just holding a rock or sitting on one can also help.

Many of us turn to professionals for help when we feel emotionally unbalanced. We may also seek out friends or family in whom we confide. Our animal companions often sense our need and offer their comfort by curling up next to us. Instinctively, we go out into nature, by the river or into the woods, to relax and replenish ourselves.

While all of the other Kingdoms can help us, the Mineral Kingdom is particularly well-suited to the necessary grounding we need so that we can regain our emotional center. Since our bodies are filled with mineral substances, it's not surprising that we need our connection to Mother Earth to maintain our equilibrium. Minerals balance and tune us so that we can complete our spiritual and physical work. They assist us in bridging the gap between the higher realms and the Earth, allowing us to integrate fully our mental, physical, and spiritual selves.

A Message From
The Overlighting Deva
Of The Mineral Kingdom

*I AM THE GUARDIAN OF THE MINERAL KINGDOM
THROUGHOUT THE UNIVERSE. I AM ALSO THE MOST
ANCIENT OF ALL THE GUARDIANS OF THE DIFFERENT
PHYSICAL BEINGS ON OUR BELOVED PLANET EARTH.*

I am the Steward of the stones upon which you walk, the mountains you climb, the soil in which you plant, the gemstones you wear, the volcanoes you watch erupt.

In my journey toward wholeness, I have moved from the physical stone body of the minerals I oversee, into pure essence or energy. I am an entity that no longer has a corporeal body.

I care for each mineral under my guidance much like a loving grandparent would care for you. Humans are the adopted grandchildren of the Mineral Kingdom. We are concerned about your welfare and want to help you in any way we can, individually and collectively.

Earth, your home, is a giant rock. The body of the planet is a collective of Mineral Kingdom lifeforms. We share this planet with you as conscious, living entities. You are our sisters and brothers and we love you. Only our form is different. Our essence is the same—Divine Energy—the protoplasm of the Universe.

WE ARE THE WITNESSES. We, of the Mineral Kingdom, are the observers and recorders of history, the witnesses of change. We have spent millions of years watching the course of Earth's evo-

35

lution. We have had an advantage over other Kingdoms in seeing the big picture. Our existence has been structured so that we have a unique, overview perspective.

Over the millennia we have seen much that you need to know. We will not bore you with a history lesson of dates and places. We want to share, instead, our observations of the human condition, your relationship to each other, to other entities, and to the Earth itself. The Universe has appointed us as your elders. We have been instructed to guide you to a greater understanding of the constructive and destructive aspects of human nature.

THE NEW MILLENNIUM: A TIME FOR US TO SPEAK. A predestined time was established when the Mineral Kingdom would reach out and connect with our human brothers and sisters. We were programmed vibrationally and energetically, that before the New Millennium dawned, we would communicate with the human collective. Since that time in our very ancient past when we all separated from the One Spark and individuated into our unique sparks, we have looked forward to this moment. Now is the time to speak.

This is a time of great fluctuation upon the planet. There have been and will be great physical changes. Earthquakes, volcanoes, hurricanes, tornadoes, and tidal waves are occurring now to get your attention. The catastrophes in the physical world are symbolic of what is happening non-physically. You have heard the saying, "As above, so below." The biggest rumblings and tumblings of all are occurring on the higher energy frequency levels.

It may appear that unless there is a disaster of some sort, nothing much ever changes in the Mineral Kingdom. Nonetheless, change is constant in our realm, although, very slow by your standards. Our particular patterns of growth and energy help hold Planet Earth together.

OUR RESPONSIBILITIES. The structure of the Earth is made up of interlocking grids of form that cross several dimensions. The energy of the Mineral Kingdom provides an etheric cohesiveness—the glue necessary to hold the grids in their proper position. This positioning is critical to maintaining internal planetary stability and a dynamic tension between all planets in the solar system and the Universe.

You may wonder how we can provide this critical service to the planet if we are continually being harvested from our home deep within the Earth. Mother Earth is a living, breathing entity. She feels pain. She gets sick. She needs her body—her foundation—intact to remain in balance. How long would you last if pieces of your body were stolen? Like many other acts of extremism on the Earth plane, mining has been taken to excess. Humans do not recognize that minerals are needed below the surface to maintain the energetic and gravitational equilibrium of the planet.

But we are torn. We also have a mission with you above the surface that is very important to us too. One of the reasons that each Kingdom exists is to assist the other Kingdoms. Long ago we pledged a cooperative relationship with humans that we continue to respect. We agreed to help connect you with the Earth and balance you emotionally and spiritually. Our mission with you depends on your uprooting us. We need to be closer to you vibrationally to help on a day-to-day basis. We are saddened that this friendship has been abused. Humans in their greediness, especially for gemstones and precious metals, are destroying a necessary balance—and along with it, each

Kingdom's chances for survival.

A TIME OF GREAT CHANGE. The closer we get to the year 2000, the more the internal structure that we have been discussing will begin to alter. The shifting of Earth's tectonic plates is representative of what is happening on the etheric planes. Physical changes result from the higher level, non-physical changes, not the other way around.

You may or may not be aware that on a spiritual level, your world is polarizing itself. We will provide a visual image to help you understand. Picture a huge group of people with a particular goal gathering at one point on the Earth and the same size group with a counter purpose at the exact opposite site. Although there are no actual physical gatherings like this, there are concentrations of energy accumulating with two opposing objectives. We avoid terms like good and evil, because these dualistic descriptions are Earth-made and not Universal in nature. It would be more appropriate to say that many humans are inclined toward the Light and many others either do not have an awareness of the Light or they have rejected it.

These different camps of intention, as we will call them, each hold an energy pattern. If their amassed energies eventually collide, they will spark a reaction that will cause a a physical shifting of the Earth's axis. The possibility of axis shifting is also increased by over-mining which continually erodes and weakens the Earth's foundation.

THE END OF SEPARATION. With or without this physical shifting, a vibrational shift is intended to occur for all Earth's life-forms. When this happens, all the Kingdoms will evolve instantaneously to a higher level of illumination and understanding.

This will not be a less physical state, as you might suspect, but a more integrated physical and spiritual state. This well-balanced dyad will eliminate much of the perceived need to maintain the duality ever present in the lives of today's humans. Duality is responsible for much of the separation, intolerance, and fear surrounding you.

Over the millennia, we have seen your world change from a place of harmony and peace to one of confusion and discord. Before the Earth was so densely populated, the heartbeat of the Earth was a tuning fork for humans. If humans became emotionally off balance, they could quiet themselves and synchronize their heartbeats with that of the Earth. Now, for the most part, the cacophony of your environment drowns out Mother Earth's harmonizing and balancing tone.

You are an endangered species. Did you think that the animals and plants were the only ones in trouble? You are more vulnerable than most of them. Many of the species that are no longer on the Earth have sacrificed themselves as warnings to you. Open your eyes. You could be next.

And yet, this does not need to be a doomsday prophecy. You have Free Will. Change is always possible. Mother Earth is always eager to nurture and assist her children. She reaches out when a breeze caresses your face, a crow calls to you, water cools your toes. She is ever present and giving, the consummate provider. It is up to you to respond. Like a wise parent, she allows you to decide if you want her help.

LET US LEARN FROM ONE ANOTHER. The turning of the millennium is a time of endings and new beginnings. It marks a reordering and a reorganization of life as we know it. Nothing will remain the same. But do not be frightened or discouraged. This is very good news. It means that each of us can impact the planet for the better.

It also implies a grave responsibility. Like never before in human evolution, you must gather together. Our world is in jeopardy. To save it, speak out and act to develop a new consciousness. For the survival of all the Kingdoms, the destiny of the planet, and existence as a whole—there must be a majority of humans who are working for the highest good of Mother Earth and all her lifeforms. We and the other Kingdoms stand ready to help.

We are so grateful for this opening of communication. This is just the beginning. Each of you can communicate with us anytime you like. Draw near, kinsfolk and, at first, just listen. Sit quietly with a favorite crystal or rock. You may not hear us with your ears. Listen with your heart, your body, your mind, and your spirit.

Once that process seems comfortable, open a dialogue with us. Tell us your stories and your feelings. Help us understand what it means to be human. You have much to teach us as well. And we want to learn.

Chakras And Stones: A Partnership In Healing

KIRLIAN PHOTOGRAPHY HAS DOCUMENTED,
SCIENTIFICALLY, AN ELECTROMAGNETIC FIELD
THAT SURROUNDS ALL LIVING ENTITIES.

This energy field serves as a container to hold and maintain the integrity of the physical body. All lifeforms are composed of energy, which either builds matter or exists in a non-material form. In addition to a visible, physical body, all Earth beings also have intangible, invisible etheric bodies. These etheric bodies are in approximately the same location as the physical body, but in different dimensions. At the outermost layer of the etheric bodies is the point in space where we actually merge with the Universe.

THE AURA. Although it is invisible to most humans, some people can see a colored energy outline called an aura radiating from the body. The colors of the rainbow dance in the aura, communicating information about an individual. Those gifted enough to read the aura, can translate the colors they see into knowledge about emotional and physical health, personality, talents, and spiritual development.

THE CHAKRAS. Our etheric bodies contain major energy centers, located along an axis parallel to the spinal column of the physical body. These centers are called chakras, which means wheel or vortex. The chakras get their name from their whirling, spinning motion. It is the spinning of the chakras that creates the aura or electromagnetic field surrounding the body. Generally, a chakra spinning in a clockwise manner is considered healthy and balanced, while counter-clockwise spinning indicates the opposite.

The chakras absorb higher energy from the Universe and step it down to a usable level for us on the physical plane. Our endocrine system assists the chakras in converting these higher vibrations into accessible energy. The chakras also work individually and collectively to keep the physical, emotional, and spiritual selves functioning optimally, in harmony with one another and the Universe.

THE NEW MILLENNIUM CHAKRA. For the most part, there is agreement that there are seven major chakras and perhaps as many as hundreds of minor ones. Each chakra is associated with glands, organs, and body locations. Each has a color, a musical note or tone, and special characteristics and qualities.

Due to energy shifts triggered by the New Millennium, there is a new major chakra now forming in the human body. It is emerging as a result of emotional and spiritual changes that are consciously occurring in the human collective. After the advent of the Millennium, additional chakras will begin to materialize.

ENERGY MEETS ENERGY. The chakras and the Mineral Kingdom work cooperatively in partnership. Both are sources of energy. Both are dedicated to restoring harmony and balance in the human vehicle. Together, the Mineral Kingdom and the chakras help us counter the effects of the outer world's chaotic bombardment.

Further, the Mineral Kingdom restores equilibrium in the chakras by merging our electromagnetic field with Mother Earth's. This bridge of energy acts as a grounding device to neutralize negative and discordant energies. Unchecked, these dissonant vibrations will affect our well-being.

Where there is disharmony, the Mineral Kingdom creates stability. Where there is imbalance, minerals contribute more or less energy, as needed. If there is congestion, they clear the obstruction. If there is confusion and doubt, they console and reassure. Moreover, the Mineral Kingdom restores chemical balance, calms emotional reactions, and opens the doors to greater awareness and illumination.

In the following descriptions of the chakras and in the messages from the Mineral Kingdom, you will understand more fully the cooperative relationship of the chakras and the stones designed for your Highest Good.

FIRST CHAKRA

NAME:	Root, Base, Coccygeal
BODY LOCATION:	Base of spine
GLAND/ORGAN:	Male Reproductive Organs, Anus
COLOR:	Black, Red, Brown, Dark Gray
NOTE/TONE:	C
QUALITIES:	Grounding, Vitality, Survival, Earth Connection, Balance
STONES:	Black Tourmaline, Boji Stones®, Hematite, Obsidian, River Rock, Septarian Nodules, Smoky Quartz, Bloodstone (also Heart)

Second Chakra

NAME: Sacral, Splenic, Gonadal, Navel
BODY LOCATION: Below navel in pelvic area

GLAND/ORGAN: Female Reproductive Organs,
                      Spleen, Intestines, Bladder
COLOR: Orange
NOTE/TONE: D

QUALITIES: Creativity, Sexuality, Emotions,
                      Sociability

STONES: Coral, Orange Calcite, Sunstone,
                      Zincite

Third Chakra

NAME: Solar Plexus
BODY LOCATION: Abdominal area below the heart

GLAND/ORGAN: Spleen, Adrenals, Digestive
                      System
COLOR: Yellow, Gold
NOTE/TONE: E

QUALITIES: Personal Power, Intellect, Will,
                      Control

STONES: Amber, Golden Calcite, Tiger's
                      Eye, Rutilated Quartz (also
                      Crown)

Fourth Chakra

NAME:	Heart
BODY LOCATION:	In middle of ribcage between the breasts
GLAND/ORGAN:	Heart, Lungs
COLOR:	Green, Pink
NOTE/TONE:	F#
QUALITIES:	Love of Self and Others, Unconditional Love, Compassion, Forgiveness, Growth, Healing
STONES:	Apophyllite, Chlorite in Quartz (also Crown), Dioptase, Green Tourmaline, Kunzite, Malachite, Moldavite, Rhodochrosite, Rose Quartz, Watermelon Tourmaline

Emerging New Millennium Chakra

NAME:	Thymus
BODY LOCATION:	Between Heart and Throat
GLAND/ORGAN:	Thymus
COLOR:	Blue-Green
NOTE/TONE:	G
QUALITIES:	Self-Identity, Authenticity, Self-Discovery, Self-Awareness
STONES:	Chrysocolla, Labradorite, Turquoise

Fifth Chakra

NAME:	Throat
BODY LOCATION:	Throat area between clavicle bones
GLAND/ORGAN:	Thyroid, Parathyroid/Throat, Vocal Cords, Mouth, Ears
COLOR:	Blue
NOTE/TONE:	G#
QUALITIES:	Communication, Self-Expression, Clairaudience
STONES:	Angelite, Celestite, Kyanite, Larimar

Sixth Chakra

NAME:	Third Eye
BODY LOCATION:	Between the Eyebrows
GLAND/ORGAN:	Pituitary, Pineal/Eyes
COLOR:	Dark Blue, Indigo, Purple
NOTE/TONE:	A
QUALITIES:	Intuition, Psychic Ability, Higher Self Connection, Clairvoyance
STONES:	Azurite, Lapis Lazuli, Charoite, Sugilite

SEVENTH CHAKRA

NAME: Crown
BODY LOCATION: Top of Head
GLAND/ORGAN: Pineal, Pituitary/Brain
COLOR: Clear, White, Lavender, Purple
NOTE/TONE: B

QUALITIES: Spirituality, Divine Consciousness, Inner Peace, Clairsentience, Wisdom, Universal Connection

STONES: Amethyst, Clear Quartz, Fluorite, Lepidolite, Moonstone, Ojo Caliente Timekeepers, Selenite

Using The
Crystal
Deva Cards

The Essence Of The Crystal Deva Cards

THE SYMBOL ON EACH CARD AND THROUGHOUT THE SET IS THE ANCIENT ALCHEMIST'S SYMBOL FOR CRYSTAL.

Our history books tell us that the goal of alchemy was to change lead into gold. A more esoteric purpose, hidden from the masses, was the transformation of the Self. The Crystal Devas hope that their messages will, like the alchemy of old, facilitate transformation in your life.

SACRED NUMEROLOGY. There are forty-four *Crystal Deva Cards* in the deck. Forty-four is a Master Number, as are eleven, twenty-two, and thirty-three. In numerology, each number has a special significance and quality that it represents.

Four is the number of physical reality, the stability of the square or cube, the translation of the non-material into matter, the esoteric into the exoteric. Forty-four can be viewed as four intensified and transformed. The size and shape of each card is a repeat of this theme—the double square of Sacred Geometry. The number forty-four integrates the perfection of the Divine into the physical plane so that we can experience Heaven on Earth.

MESSAGES FOR THE NEW MILLENNIUM. Each card is imprinted with a photograph of a mineral specimen, its name, and an attribute. If you have worked with minerals before, you may have associated different qualities with them than the ones you see in this deck. Don't let that trouble you. Just like us, minerals are evolving additional dimensions to their purpose and personalities. Each individual message presented in this text reveals new, timely information about a critical aspect of human existence. The Crystal Devas and stones have chosen to impart this particular loving guidance for the Highest Good of Humankind as we face the challenges of the New Millennium.

THE ENERGY OF THE STONES. As the Devas impart their information, they pass along their essence with it. Each card and message is imbued with the energy of the mineral and is vibrating at the same frequency. For that reason, in the individual card messages, a Crystal Deva may suggest that if you don't have a stone to use in meditation, you may use the card for a similar experience.

Some of the Crystal Devas will specify certain methods of working with their stone bodies; others will not. Even if they do not verbalize it in their section, all of them recommend meditating while holding the stone or card in your hand or placing it over its companion chakra.

Another way of working with the stones is to open a dialogue with them. Quiet your mind and concentrate on the essence of the mineral. Let it fill your consciousness. In your thoughts or aloud, speak your intention to communicate. Be still and see what follows. At first, there may be nothing. But if you continue this process, you will make a connection.

As you read the messages of the Crystal Devas, you may notice that they typically say "we" and "our," instead of "I" and "my." This is because they are representing a collective. Each Crystal Deva speaks on behalf of an entire stone presence wherever it exists throughout the world.

As a result of experiencing the Mineral Kingdom through this deck, you may be drawn to acquire some crystals or mineral specimens. When inviting new mineral friends into your life, don't overlook rocks that call to you from alongside the road or a riverbed. Don't let appearances fool you—there are no ordinary rocks. All stones are sources of information, inspiration, and wisdom, not just the well-known ones. The Angel Rock—mentioned earlier—that inspired this deck, was a simple, unglamorous rock lying near a hiking trail.

Let your Higher Self direct you. It will select the cards that will help you bring clarity, peace, and fulfillment into your life. The Mineral Kingdom stands ready to help—grateful for this time of reawakening and reunion.

Working With The Crystal Deva Cards

*SINCE ANCIENT TIMES, HUMANS HAVE LOOKED FOR
A SOURCE OF WISDOM OUTSIDE OURSELVES,
FORGETTING THAT REAL KNOWLEDGE LIES WITHIN US
AS AN INHERITANCE FROM THE UNIVERSE.*

The *Crystal Deva Cards* are an oracle designed for tapping into Universal Wisdom and Truth. Their messages are intended to guide you on your Earthly sojourn—providing clarity, hope, and encouragement. As part of this Divine Guidance system, your Higher Self chooses the cards that you need for growth, learning, and self-empowerment.

Whenever you work with the cards, prepare to enter a sacred space. You are about to open yourself to Divine Counsel. Quiet your mind and body. Reverently appreciate this moment.

You may have a specific question in mind, or simply, a general request for guidance. Hold this thought in your mind as you prepare to receive information. Shuffle the cards at least three times, and fan them out before you. Your eye will attract you to the card(s) your Higher Self is directing you to pick. There are never any inappropriate choices. Even if you do not immediately identify with the message of a card or spread, continue to think about it during your day or meditate on it. A recognition of its significance will come to you.

You may decide to draw one card to receive a daily message. You may use the Chakra Tuning for balance and awareness. Or you may want to work with the card spreads, recommended to assist in your discovery of Self by addressing particular life questions, issues, or areas of concern. As you become more familiar with the *Crystal Deva Cards*, develop new methods of working with them.

Seven ways to get started

Daily Guidance

>Inspiration To Carry With You
>Throughout The Day

Chakra Tuning

>Developing Self-awareness To Uncover And
>Balance Critical Life Issues

The Spreads

>Cave Spread: Introspection
>
>The Volcano Spread: Transformation
>
>Island Spread: Tolerance
>
>Mother Earth Spread: Healing
>
>Mountain Spread: Higher Consciousness

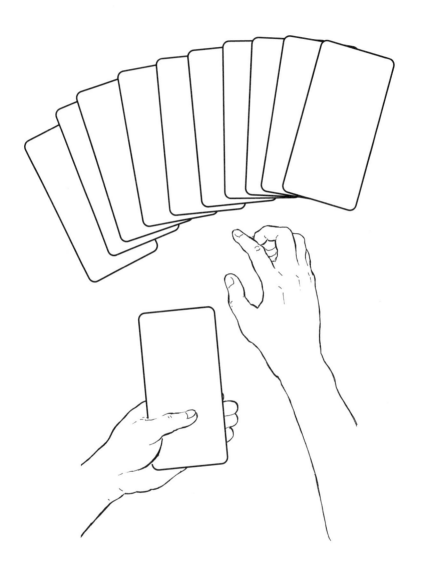

Daily Guidance

Every day, each of us has questions about a variety of life issues. It's not always possible, or comfortable, to share our innermost concerns with someone else. We, as human personalities, sometimes have trouble finding the right answers to our questions. But there's a source of information available to us that we can count on without hesitation—our Higher Self. Our Higher Self is part of who we are and our connection to the Universe. If we listen and watch, it will provide the instruction that we need.

As part of a daily ritual, or whenever you feel it's appropriate, prepare yourself for a special time of communication with your Higher Self. Respectfully request that the information you receive be for the Highest Good of all concerned. Meditate on your question for a few moments in a peaceful, relaxed state. Be willing to give your attention to the message that is offered even if it raises uncomfortable feelings or resistance within you.

Draw a card to receive guidance for the day. If you want more information, draw other cards to expand the message of the first. Your question may begin in a generalized fashion and become more specific as you draw other cards. The order in which the cards are drawn may be a clue as to which issue should be examined first, before going on to the next.

The cards may bring more clarity to an issue that you have been thinking about. They may confront you with a concept that you need to explore. They may offer enlightenment, reassurance, or balance. Your Higher Self has answered your desire for self-knowledge and direction. Each time you acknowledge its presence in your life by listening to it, it will forge a stronger link with you, connecting you to Universal Truth.

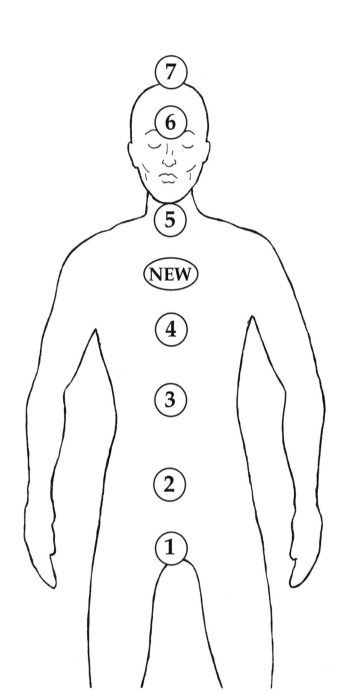

Chakra Tuning

DEVELOPING SELF-AWARENESS TO
UNCOVER AND BALANCE CRITICAL LIFE ISSUES.

The seven major chakras (and a new, emerging one) are sacred spaces within the human body. Each holds an energy that is designed to help you vibrationally accommodate the challenges of Earthly existence.

The chakras work to invigorate and heal the physical self, calm and balance the emotional self, and open and attune the spiritual self. Their mission is to assist the life process, so that human beings may return to the Divine Source, fully illuminated and integrated.

Working with the chakras can pinpoint underlying issues that have not yet been resolved. This exercise is specifically designed to reveal these areas and help balance and heal them. You can find out more about yourself by exploring the significance of each chakra. Self-awareness is the key to self-realization.

If you feel unbalanced and off center, you may wish to use this exercise for chakra tuning.

1. First, **quiet your mind** and body and enter a receptive state.

2. Next, **shuffle the cards and choose one** to discover the chakra and issues that need special attention. The card you pick will shed light on how you are connecting to the basic life concepts

represented by the energy of this chakra.

3. Then, with the cards face up, **select more cards**—as many as you like—associated with that particular chakra. (See the following list for chakra-related cards.)

4. **Surround yourself** (sitting or lying) with these cards in a circle or other geometrically-shaped grid that appeals to you. The cards will create a healing energy field around you.

5. To intensify the energy field, **add any actual stones** you may own to the grid that relate to the same chakra.

6. Visualize the chakra filled with white light, spinning, and opening to the energy field. Allow it to drink in the nourishment of the energy emitted by the cards and stones. **Spend some time in meditation** soaking up this essence. This experience will help you gain a new understanding and balancing of the issues which have presented themselves.

7. As with any meditation, you'll sense when your chakra has absorbed all the energy it can. You'll know when it's time to **conclude this session.**.

8. After your meditation time, **choose a stone,** if you have one, that is associated with the the chakra with which you've been working. **Carry it with you** throughout the day and **sleep with it** under your pillow at night.

THE CHAKRAS AND THEIR CARDS

FIRST
Root chakra—Earth connection, balance, and basic survival needs
(Cards 6, 7, 8, 19, 29, 33, 37, 38)

SECOND
Sacral chakra—your creative, sexual, and social selves
(Cards 14, 31, 40, 44)

THIRD
Solar Plexus chakra—personal power and will
(Cards 1, 17, 41, 35)

FOURTH
Heart chakra—love of self and others, compassion, and unconditional love
(Cards 4, 7, 11, 15, 18, 20, 26, 27, 32, 34, 43)

NEW
Thymus chakra—self-identity and authenticity
(Cards 12, 22, 42)

FIFTH
Throat chakra—your ability and willingness to communicate
(Cards 3, 9, 21, 24)

SIXTH
Third Eye chakra—openness to intuition and psychic abilities
(Cards 5, 23, 10, 39)

SEVENTH
Crown chakra—your connection to spirituality, peace, and the Universe
(Cards 2, 11, 13, 16, 25, 28, 30, 35, 36)

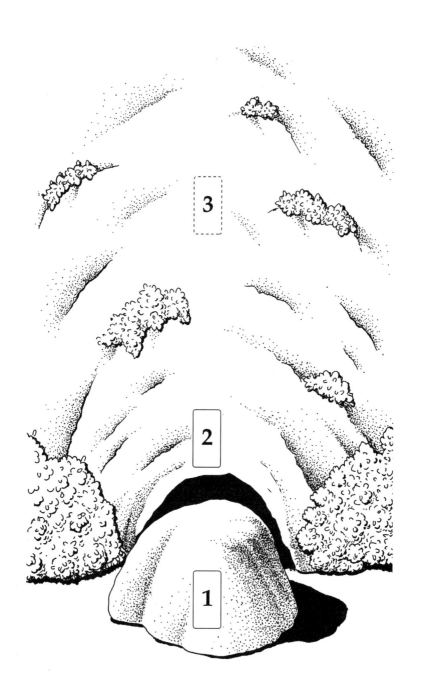

The Cave Spread: Introspection

Caves are places of great mystery and history, and have much to teach us. When you enter a cave, you go into the heart of the earth. When you use this card spread, you journey to the heart of the situation about which you have questions.

The cave experience offered here harbors no dangerous drop-offs or ferocious beasts. It is a protected place where discovery poses no threats. This cave is a rock womb that shelters and provides a safe haven for learning and experience.

The womb experience is a transition state where we prepare for an entirely new life. This card spread will reveal key issues to contemplate as you make decisions about any potential under-taking—a new relationship, career, educational pursuit, lifestyle change, or spiritual quest.

1. The first card is the **Obstacle** card. As you begin to enter your cave, you find a large boulder barring your way. This card reveals the issue that is blocking your progress and obscuring your perspective. You must create a way to eliminate this roadblock. What needs to happen in your life before you can move forward?

2. The second card is the **Entrance** card. Once you have passed by the barrier, you find yourself in the cave's entryway. To access

the wonder of the cave, you must put aside any doubts and enter it. To access your own personal mysteries, you must also bravely venture inside yourself. This card indicates what you need for emotional support to help you reach your decision. Contemplate its meaning before selecting the final card.

3. The third card is the **Inner Sanctum** card. You have successfully reached the center of the cave. To face any situation honestly, there must be a time of solitude, contemplation, and introspection. The bear always chooses a cave for its time of hibernation and preparation. Follow its example. This last card will suggest the key issue to consider before making your important decision.

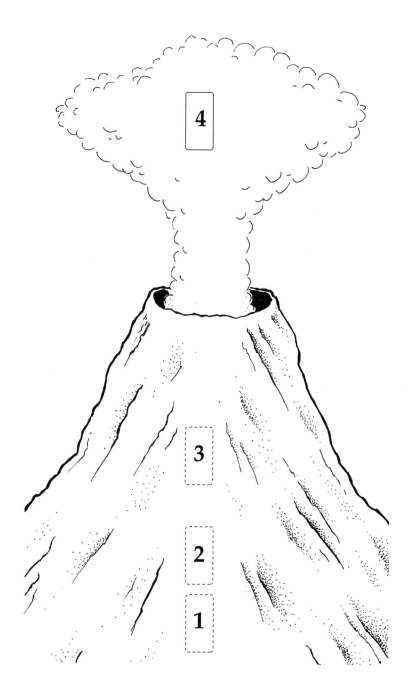

The Volcano Spread: Transformation

The lava of a volcano is a symbol of our potential for movement and change. In your life, when an issue forces its way to the surface, it's trying to tell you something. Is this the time to do something about it—or your life, in general? If so, now may be the perfect opportunity for a metamorphosis.

The volcano performs a valuable service. It provides a vehicle for the Earth to send its lifeblood to the surface to cleanse and purify. Lava destroys whatever it touches, to make way for the new. Change often requires the destruction of outdated belief systems to create new ones that reflect who you are currently. This card spread provides the tools to facilitate change in your life—to allow your new self to rise.

1. The first card is the **Gathering** card. Underneath the base of the volcano, pools of magma accumulate to provide the volume of force needed to propel the lava upward. The card that you choose will suggest a resource that you need to collect prior to your journey.

2. The second card is the **Activation** card. To fuel the process of growth, the energy you have amassed must be ignited. This card's message will direct you as to what is required to kindle your own internal flame—to arouse you from your time of

anticipation into action.

3. The third card is the **Propulsion** card. The lava begins its journey upward through the core of the volcano. What is at the core of your situation? What quality expressed by this card will propel you into the metamorphosis you desire?

4. The fourth and final card is the **Eruption** card. Lava is over-flowing the mouth of the volcano ready to complete its purpose of cleansing and change. This last card will explain the final step necessary for you to take to complete your transformation.

The Island Spread:
Tolerance

The shipwrecked fictional character living on an island is a symbol of isolation and loneliness. He has no choice. The rest of us do.

Why do we detach ourselves from others? Sometimes we participate in self-imposed isolation because we feel vulnerable or afraid. Being alone is fine, but seclusion based on fear is not healthy. The Universe's plan is for all of us to live interactively and in harmony with one another.

We fear others because they are different. We don't know them well enough to anticipate their unfamiliar behavior or customs. Our inability to pigeonhole them into our comfortable structure unnerves us. We feel we must be cautious. After all, they're unpredictable.

Differences in philosophy, behavior, and appearances should not be viewed as a threat. If we erase these fabricated barriers through an appreciation, rather than an apprehension, of diversity, we can move out of our exile and into the light.

Intolerance is not only outwardly directed, it strikes much closer to home. Our lack of acceptance of others is a reflection of the disappointment and rejection we feel toward ourselves. If we hate our own imperfections and eccentricities, we won't be able to see beyond them in others. Being different is not bad. Being different is a Divine gift called uniqueness. Its special quality has been distorted because of our obsessive need for sameness and belongingness. We can belong in the truest sense, happy and fulfilled, by contributing our uniqueness to the harmonious family of Earth.

Open your heart and view all lifeforms as your family. Move from a position of judgment or apathy into one of acceptance and caring. When we no longer need to protect and insulate ourselves, we can learn from each other and experience the warmth and support of fellowship.

Use this card spread if you are feeling critical, intolerant, or unforgiving of yourself, another individual, or a generalized group. The Island spread is dedicated to acceptance, spiritual cooperation, and the rejection of polarization.

Polarization is a disharmony of spirit that breeds hatred and intolerance. The message here is to to open your heart, in kindness, to yourself and all those around you—those of different races, sizes, abilities, sexual preferences, belief systems, or species. Acceptance is the key to harmony within yourself and in your relationships with all other beings.

1. The first card is the **Mirror** card. Deep within is your internal mirror of truth. Look into it and ask "What stands in the way of my acceptance of myself or others?" Let the card you draw direct you in understanding how you relate to this concept.

2. The second card is the **Protection** card. We all set up shields to protect ourselves. Sometimes, our fear exhibits itself in bigotry or separatism. We are afraid of those who are not like us. We are also afraid of the unknown, unpredictable parts of our-

selves. What does this card tell you about your own protective devices?

3. The third card is the **Opening** card. If we let go of fear, we can open our hearts and our eyes in love and acceptance. We can begin to see without judgment the good that lies underneath the tough, distancing exteriors of others. What message does this card bring to help you work on this challenging task?

4. The fourth card is the **Vulnerability** card. Once we realize that all of us are the same, and not different, it is easier to let our guard down. To make oneself accessible to others is to drop layers of fear and barriers of isolation. You gain freedom from the prison of alienation and loneliness you have created for yourself. How can this card help you?

5. The fifth card is the **Reconciliation** card. We were always meant to be together. We were intended to see beyond the external costumes and masks to the Divinity within. Diversity is a test of, and lesson in, tolerance. Learn from it. Let this last card, combined with the other four, guide you to a new understanding and love of your Earthly family and yourself.

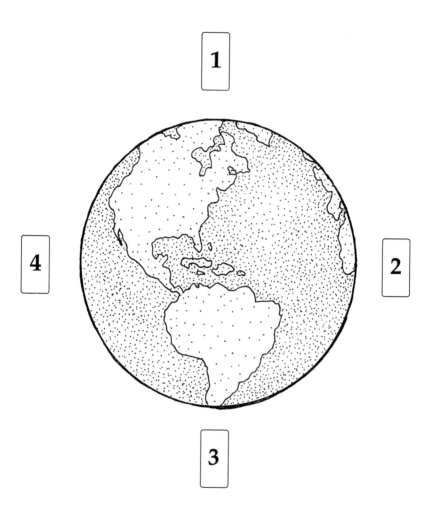

The Mother Earth Spread: Healing

ALLEVIATING PHYSICAL, EMOTIONAL, AND SPIRITUAL SUFFERING

Why have you selected the spread for healing? You may be look-ing for healing of a physical illness or an emotional problem. You may need to forgive someone for abusive treatment or neglect. Or do you want to forgive yourself for something you have done to another? Have you lost a loved one to divorce or death? Does a valuable friendship need mending? Maybe you are in pain because you have neglected or forgotten your spiritual path. Healing is available to you, waiting to make you whole again.

Although physical suffering can be devastating, emotional and spiritual wounds often last long beyond the effects of a bodily trauma. Trust Mother Earth to help you. She is the great healer. She has given us every resource for the integration of our physi-cal, emotional, and spiritual selves. Perhaps her greatest gift is that of facilitating internal balance, returning us to a place of calm and peace within. She has provided us with the beautiful, healing presence of Nature to restore our well-being. In Mother Earth's loving arms, we are comforted, reassured, and healed.

Tell her what you need and ask her for her guidance. Select four cards as you describe the area(s) which need to be healed.

1. The first card is the card of **Recognition.** Look deep within to determine what truly causes your suffering. Let this card clarify

this issue for you.

2. The second card is the card of **Permission.** You must consent for healing to occur. You must be willing for your pain to surface so that Mother Earth can assist you. Permit her to lovingly nurture you as you unburden yourself of your sorrow or fear. The card you pick will provide clues as to how she can help you and how you can help yourself.

3. The third card is the card of **Liberation.** After you have confronted the issue that troubles you, allow Mother Earth to surround the energy that needs to be healed and release it to the Universe for transmutation. We often hold on to painful memories because they are all that remain of a former relationship, life, or Self. If healing is to occur, we must let the pain go. Once released to the Universe, this energy will return to you like a boomerang, but in a different form. That which had formerly held despondency and pessimism, now is filled with confidence and hope. What does this particular card tell you?

4. The fourth card is the card of **Restoration.** The Universal Energy that has flowed into your life contains all the necessary ingredients for healing—unconditional love, forgiveness, and acceptance. You are now equipped to heal the unresolved issues which have existed in your life. Let this last card sum up the four you have selected as a blueprint for healing.

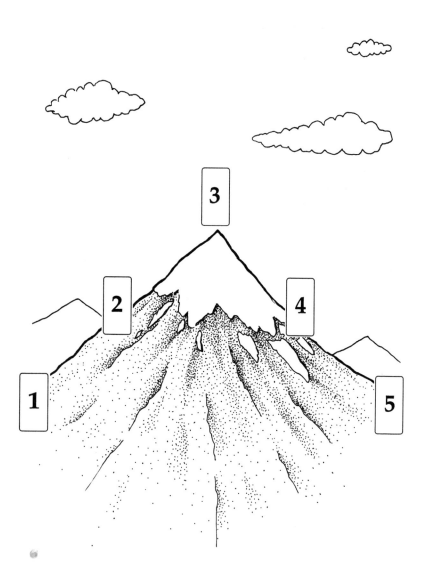

The Mountain Spread: Higher Consciousness

INTEGRATING SPIRITUALITY INTO DAILY LIFE

When you decide to climb a mountain, you need strength, endurance, and commitment. In addition, you need supplies that will sustain you on your journey—food, water, appropriate clothing. The journey to Higher Consciousness requires similar resources.

When the time feels right to raise questions about your spiritual life, listen to the Will of the Divine and not that of your personality. Like the unscaled mountain, your spiritual journey is a walk into the Unknown. Prepare yourself. Don't start off impulsively or without regard for your welfare. Carefully consider this undertaking. This expedition requires bravery, resolve, and confidence.

This passage is a transition from all that you have been before to an entirely different self. It is the journey of a lifetime. Let the cards in this spread express the concepts that will make your encounter with Higher Consciousness possible.

1. The first card is the **Commencement** card. No successful journey can occur without a proper beginning. To accomplish your goals, you must gather the necessary essentials. This card will guide you in what you need.

2. The second card is the **Endurance** card. Along the path up the

mountain are pitfalls—fatigue, failing resolve, fear, apathy. Let the message of this card help you keep your commitment to yourself.

3. The third card is the **Summit** card. Here is the place of Vision Quests, where we come face to face with our hopes, fears, and the Unknown. Although we must confront ourselves alone, there is always unseen help available. What issue will you encounter as you reach the top?

4. The fourth card is the **Transition** card. You are now assimilating the information you have gained in your solitude on the mountaintop and determining how it pertains to your life in the real world. What are your challenges?

5. The fifth card is the **Integration** card. You have travelled to the realms of a different plane. You have left the material and gone to the spiritual. Now it is time to bring your spiritual guidance back and integrate it into your physical life. This is the goal of the Universe for those of us on Earth—the perfect balance of the physical, emotional, and spiritual. This final card will guide you in remembering your spiritual lessons while facing the challenges of the Earthly plane.

Messages
Of The
Crystal
Devas

1

Amber

NON-RESISTANCE

Amber

NON-RESISTANCE

Chakra: Solar Plexus
Color: Gold

The Earth is a school for cosmic learning, for soul growth, for evolution. Life is continuously presenting instruction through experience. Sometimes, the lessons are hard, filled with sorrow and pain. Perhaps a loved one leaves you through death, or to be with another.

In the midst of your despair, it may be difficult to recognize that there is something to be learned from the ordeal you are facing. Sometimes the greatest lesson of the many that this experience brings may be that of encouraging non-resistance—letting go.

Long after physical separation occurs, you may spend years or decades holding on emotionally. You may be clinging to a reality that no longer exists except for the energy you supply to it. You are unable to move forward because you are stuck like the insect in the Amber.

Unlike the insect, you have the power to release yourself from your bondage. Your resistance is your prison. Your resistance to what has happened is your denial of the truth. It is time to free yourself. Spread your spirit wings and fly. Rise above what is anchoring you so tightly and keeping you Earthbound.

It is non-resistance that allowed us to change our identity from one Kingdom to another. We start our life in the Plant Kingdom, as the lifeblood of the tree. As we move from a liquid to a solid state, we undergo a transmutation and become a bridge between the Plant and Mineral Kingdoms. We are the embodiment of adaptability and what it can accomplish. When the Mineral Kingdom opened its heart to us and adopted a foreigner into its family, it served as a further example of non-resistance.

Why has our card called to you today? Are you feeling stuck in some old emotion or situation? Perhaps you are resisting a change that you know you should make. Maybe you are being stubborn about an issue and need to compromise. Decide how the concept of resistance relates to your current life.

Once you know where your resistance lies, sit and meditate on our golden color. We work with the Solar Plexus, the representation of the Sun in the human body. Let us melt the rigidity and fear that perpetuate your situation so that you can move through it. Become the sap. Feel the liquid state you become—flowing, unimpeded—pushing through any obstruction. Move whatever has been in your way, out of your way.

Feel your heart and all your chakras move into a liquid, unbound state. Energy moves up your chakra system through your crown into the heavens beyond and down again through the soles of your feet into the Earth below. Flowing. No rigidity can exist in this state. You are one with all.

Even in our solid mineral state, we are always moving, pulsing, flowing. So are you. It is only your attachments and resistance that bind you up. Welcome the energy and help of the Universe to travel through you.

When the Universe presents its education, it has no intention of causing you pain or harming you. It is actually you, yourself, who have developed the lesson plan. The Universe only implements what you have set into motion for your own growth. Non-resistance is one way of dealing with the circumstances that life presents.

Resistance makes change impossible. Allowing is the key. Shift from an immobile state to one of malleability. Move freely and quickly through life's lessons absorbing all that they offer you. Allow yourself to see clearly what is occurring. Move beyond the emotionality and into the spirituality. Learn. You are the teacher. You are the student. Join the Divine Flow.

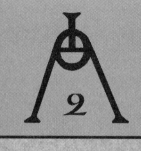

Amethyst

DIVINE CONSCIOUSNESS

Amethyst

DIVINE CONSCIOUSNESS

Chakra: Crown
Color: Purple

Your link to the Divine is close at hand. It is not in some remote region of the heavens as you suspect. It is within each of you. You are never far away from Divine Guidance, for it is part of you. You *are* the Divine—a spark of All-Knowingness that permeates the Universe.

You are connected to a web of Light that flows throughout the Universe. It is part of every creature, familiar or alien. In your own right, you are powerful. When you merge with the Source, you have the full authority and wisdom of the Universe at your disposal.

Throughout time, we and the other Kingdoms have used signals of communication to reach out to you, our human brothers and sisters. One of these is color, another sound. The language of both is based on the vibrational frequency it transmits, touching into the human psyche in a particular way. In the human body, color, sound, and all vibration is filtered through and registered in the chakra system.

We are a tool for accessing Divine Consciousness. We work with the Crown chakra in drawing Cosmic Energy into the body to be used on the physical plane. Within meditation, if held in the hand, or placed on top of the head, we can help open this chakra.

There is nothing magical about this process. Vibrational frequencies are keys. They can unlock rooms to the Self that have been long forgotten. You may not be aware that these treasure vaults are inside you. Now you have access. You have safeguarded the riches within until a time when you could make the best use of them. NOW is the time.

From the beginning of time, royalty and clergy have embraced deep purple to wear in their ceremonial robes. The Ancients chose our stones to decorate their breastplates and crowns. These adornments were not simply signs of wealth and nobility. They were carefully executed sacred geometrical instruments for the gathering of energy, strength, and power.

The humans of long ago understood the role that vibration plays in creating a desired effect. Our presence helped them to open more fully to the wisdom of Universal Consciousness.

Although largely lost to modern understanding, in ancient times, we were recognized as an antenna to the Intelligence of the Cosmos. We serve as a tuning fork that calibrates the body to receive Divine Consciousness. Just like the satellite dishes in common use today, we open the Crown chakra like a bowl, a receiver to the stars.

In our cluster form, we can be used as a tool for acupressure, activating subtle energy centers in the physical and etheric bodies. Because our points are sharp, first cover the body with a cloth or towel. Blockages, especially of a spiritual nature, can be released by gently manipulating the cluster over the skin surface.

There are pockets within the Earth that hold giant, boulder-sized crystals of Amethyst. They are waiting for the time when they will serve as power centers for the Earth's tuning, like the Pyramids and other Sacred Sites. There will be a synchronized timing schedule that will cause our Brothers and Sisters to rise from below and push their way through the Earth's crust to the surface.

If you have drawn our card today, it is time to realize that Divine Consciousness is your birthright, no less than the ancient Divine Right of Kings. It is a limitless source of power that you may tap into. Are you aware of these special resources at your disposal?

You may have forgotten that Universal assistance is open to you. You may have become bogged down in day-to-day Earthly business. Sometimes, business is just busy-ness that is part of the comings and goings of a active life. If you feel out of touch with your Divine potential, we will help you tune your vibration to easily access the Source.

One of the tragedies of human life as we view it is that you incorrectly see yourself as so alone, with no help available. The feelings of isolation and separateness that you feel are an illusion. You have been deluded and manipulated into believing this lie by those who have been in control of the planet over the millennia.

The deceit is at an end. Now is the time for Re-Union with the Divine. You have always been connected and now you will remember. Consciously reach out to claim the blessed companionship that is yours.

Live a limitless life. Your horizons stretch across the Universe. Each of you is a Queen or King. Dear one, you have a royal soul and we bow to you.

3

Angelite

SELF-EXPRESSION

Angelite

SELF-EXPRESSION

Chakra: Throat
Color: Blue

Angels are your unseen friends, always at your side. They are your constant guardians and helpmates. Many of you were incorrectly taught that Angels are accessible to you only when you die. Angels are ever near and available to you.

Most of you have probably had experiences with Angels in your life. Perhaps some miracle occurred whereby you were protected in an accident. Maybe you were stranded with no apparent chance for help when someone happened along. These may have been Angelic interactions.

Angels are not only in Heaven, as you picture them. Some Angels have volunteered for service on the Earth plane. They walk among you everyday. You may be working with the Angelic Kingdom, yourself, although you may not be consciously aware of it. If you bring joy, hope, friendship, and laughter into the lives of others, you may be an Angel.

Other lifeforms have also volunteered to work in an Angelic capacity on Earth. There are representatives in all the Kingdoms. We are one of these. We are not the only mineral working with the Angelic Kingdom in this way. Perhaps others in the Mineral Kingdom will share their Angelic work with you.

It is our honor to speak with you, human sister or brother. Our color and name are intended to remind you of the accessibility of Angels. Our color is that of the Heavens, the blue sky above you. Our name is significant because we work closely with the Angelic Kingdom in a cooperative mission here on Earth.

As a messenger from the Angelic Kingdom who has chosen to work from the Earth plane, we do all that we can to help the Earth function optimally. You are aware that the Earth's physical and spiritual bodies are under great stress. The continuing pollution and degradation of the Earth's land, oceans, and atmosphere present a tremendous challenge for all of us working for the Earth's good. The Earth is a great Spirit and will survive, although many of its lifeforms may not.

For the World to remain a viable environment to support life, there must be a cooperation among the Kingdoms, an encircling of the planet with a united front of strength and love. The Animal, Plant, and Mineral Kingdoms have supported the Earth from the beginning. It is the main goal of our group missions here.

There was a time when the Human Kingdom worked with the other Kingdoms continuously. However, over the millennia with your individual pursuits and preoccupations, you forgot that our first directive was to protect our Mother, the Earth.

We do not chastise or blame you for this. Please do not misunderstand. We know that forgetting was important to your learning and growth, individually, and as a species. Remembering is also part of that plan. All Kingdoms have diversions which lead us from our paths. Ultimately, we return in a fuller way. It is the way of evolution.

We call upon you now, brothers and sisters, to use this remarkable talent of Self-Expression. The Throat chakra is the center of expression and humans are particularly gifted in using the voice and words. Whether you are more comfortable using words orally or in written form, we ask you to speak out as an advocate for Planet Earth and all its inhabitants. Be an example for your fellow humans and also for some non-terrestrials who are gathering here for the Millennium. There is Universal interest in this next step of enlightenment for the Planet.

Help others realize that for Life to continue, there must be a recognition that all of us here are kindred spirits and family. There is only the appearance of separation because of the different physical bodies we have. Think of the difficulty you have in accepting that other humans of different colors, nationalities, and abilities are your brothers and sisters. It must be especially difficult for you to accept other Kingdoms as part of your family.

Talk with others about the need to honor each other and the Earth. You may think that if all chemicals, air pollution, and landfills were to disappear from the planet, we would have no more problems. In actually, these are small problems. What is damaging Planet Earth and all the Kingdoms more than anything else is a lack of Honor and Respect.

This may be a new concept for you. All entities need love for survival. Love nourishes each and every one of us. We miss your love. And the being, Planet Earth, is horribly ill from lack of it. Help us heal Her and ourselves.

Your self-expression is more than just your voice. You have many methods of expression available to you. All of you have talents. If you are a carpenter or plumber, dedicate your time to projects like Habitat for Humanity and help build a home for those who would not have otherwise had one.

If you are a hairdresser, go to the homes of shut-ins or to nursing homes and give these people a happier outlook on life. If you are an artist, create works of art that inspire the human spirit. If you are gifted at teaching, whether a professional or not, do not let your talents lie idle. Teach what you know. Use it to express love.

Whatever talents you have been given, GIVE BACK. It is not too late to change the World. You have great power in your self-expression. It is one of the reasons you were created. It is through self-expression that you evolve. And so does the Universe. New insights, inventions, technological and spiritual advances move the Universe into bold expressions of growth.

If you drew our card today, you may be looking for new means of expression. Although your desire is great, you may be reluctant to express yourself in an unfamiliar way. Many of you have been criticized or ridiculed while trying out new skills or using your talents. Unless you can be sure of success, you would rather not risk embarrassment. This fear of failure robs you of your life.

You never know what may fulfill you or be a contribution until you try it. Please do not pass up an opportunity because of fear. We promise that the rewards are worth the risk.

We salute you, Human Kinspeople. Be our voice. Speak for us and tell humans everywhere that our global family needs you all. Join us in saving the Earth.

4

Apophyllite

GENTLENESS

Apophyllite

GENTLENESS

Chakra: Heart
Color: Light Green

An act of gentleness is a bold statement of love. It is a sign that you are able to move beyond concerns of vulnerability or rejection to open your heart to another in kindness.

Why is gentleness so often misunderstood? Many humans are reluctant to be gentle because they equate gentleness with weakness. Experience may have taught them that if they do not have a tough, hard exterior, others will take advantage of them. Your concerns have merit. Your world has become a cruel place. There are those who do not respect a gentle soul. What should you do if you are faced with their contempt?

We suggest—be who you are. You are not the stereotypic tough guy of your movies. You are a gentle Angel with your feet planted upon Mother Earth. If you have lost touch with this part of yourself, you can reclaim it. It is not gone, only lying dormant.

We work with the Heart chakra to help you get reacquainted with the gentle self you may have felt you needed to suppress. Touch into your gentleness by putting our card or a piece of light green Apophyllite against your heart. Feel the waves of gentleness sweep over your being. As you allow this sweet sensation to wash over you, you feel all tension and stress disappear.

All the energy you have been using to protect yourself can now be used for other purposes.

If some people abuse you for your gentleness, there are so many more who will love you for it. Your world needs gentling. Think of how good it feels when a kind friend touches you gently. It is just as soothing to have your spirit caressed in the same way.

How can you become a gentle person? Allow your heart to open. A wave of love and benevolence will radiate from it that will reach into all parts of the Universe. As with all energy, that which you send out comes back to you, boomerang-style. And while it is on its trip, it touches all life with tenderness.

You have a saying, "If not me, who? If not now, when?" Are you willing to dedicate yourself to creating a gentler, loving world? Without gentleness, humankind is doomed. If there are survivors in a world without gentleness, would you want to be one of them? We do not mean to frighten you, but you must be educated as to the importance of this vibration of kindness and love to your continued existence.

Help us in sending a message to all star voyagers and to all the other home bases for life in the Universe. Let it be known from this day forward, Planet Earth is the home of gentleness. Anyone who travels here will be treated with kindness, love, and respect.

Gentleness has as its constant companions, tolerance, compassion, and generosity. Hate and fear can not thrive where these virtues exist. Gentleness can heal Planet Earth.

You have chosen our card today because gentleness calls to you. Its song is winding its way into your heart. You may hope to shed your fearful protective garments in favor of a relaxed gentle self. You may feel a need to be gentler with yourself or others. Perhaps you are in a relationship, personal or professional, where you are suffering abuse of some kind. Your selection of this card indicates your decision to honor yourself by making whatever changes are necessary to live a life full of love, respect, and joy.

What shape will your contribution of gentleness take? When someone sends hate-filled words or energy your way, will you neutralize this negativity by sending love? Will you remember how important gentleness is to the formation of young spirits the next time a child's behavior exasperates you? Will you be kinder to your mate and friends when something they say pushes one of your hot buttons?

You are now aware of your gentle self. Please tap into the tenderness inside you. Accept the responsibility that whatever you send out affects the Whole. Your gentleness will register in the collective unconscious and positively contribute to the well-being of all. Every living entity will be gentler because of you. We bless you in your giving.

Azurite

Inner Guidance

Azurite

INNER GUIDANCE

Chakra: Third Eye
Color: Dark Blue

What you see with your physical eyes appears to be real. Often, this reality is only an illusion. Discerning the difference depends largely on *In-sight*.

Insight is a precursor to wisdom. Your intuition is one of the most valuable tools at your disposal for discovering the Truth. Deep within the cavity of your brain is a cave of inner wisdom. Its position behind the eyes symbolically represents that which is seen with the Inner Eye. This is the location of the Third Eye chakra.

Our offering to you is connection to insight—the ability to see clearly and accurately. Insight is sight focused inwardly—trusting and relying on your inner guidance.

Azurite operates like a tuning fork that equilibrates and balances the Third Eye—the place of clairvoyance, or clear seeing. But beyond the Third Eye, we connect with higher chakras outside the body that assist humans with a link with Divine Consciousness. This link facilitates the ability of clear knowing—clairsentience.

Clairsentience is a confirmation of the truth surrounding any issue. For example, you may wonder whether or not you should proceed in a certain direction or trust a particular person. With this inner truth at your disposal, you are always equipped to move forward with guidance to take whatever action is needed.

Are you trusting your intuition? Are you taking the time to tune in? To Intuit means to go Into It. The *it* is your Self. It may take some practice to quiet your mind and locate that quite, deep place inside. But once you do, answers will come effortlessly and quickly.

Trust your gut level feeling. That feeling in the Solar Plexus is tied directly to your third eye, the place of clear seeing. When you feel something in your gut, you are getting a physical response to and a confirmation of your inner knowing—your intuition.

If you have drawn this card today, you are making a request to explore the true source of your knowing—your intuition. You may be seeking assistance in making some important decision. Take a look at who is guiding you. Is it your inner self or outer influences? Rely on your insight to help resolve any confusion you feel.

Focus your eyes on the dark blue of our card or our stone body. If you look intently, the blue may begin to swirl like a vortex, pulling you deep within yourself. Our color and the color energy of your Third Eye chakra are the same. This is an example of the outer world reflecting the inner. Not just in color, but with the same energy and purpose. As Above, so Below. As Within, so Without.

We extend an invitation to you to travel the narrow passages back to the cave where revelation and understanding are one. Here is a place where you may escape the outer world and find a quiet refuge within. This is the place of answers, of inner knowing.

The pineal gland in the brain, located near the Third Eye, is connected to our work. Little is known about this gland. It is a sacred spot in the body opening the door to the Hall of the Akashic Records. The Akashic Records is a repository, an ancient chronicle that holds the history of all Humankind, of all Beingkind as well. Every event in each entity's life is recorded. The knowledge of all time is there. It is a library of experience.

We can help you open the door to the Akashic Records so that you may gain insight into your history. From this information, what you learn about past events will shed light on your present and your possible futures.

There is a condition under which someone may approach the Hall of the Akashic Records. One must enter with a pure heart, vowing to use the information gathered there for the betterment of the Whole. If this tenet is disregarded, you will forget the information you have gained and it will be lost to you.

Always on ready reserve for you is a depth of wisdom that will guide your steps truly and steer you to the right course. This is not a time in your life to ask for the opinions of others. This is a time to go within and gather your own sacred tools of wisdom. Using Inner Sight, you can see clearly from a Soul perspective and decisions can be reached easily. Along with needed answers and information, comes a sense of peace regarding any action you need to take.

Acting on your intuition allows spiritual inner guidance to be translated into insight. With insight, you access mental clarity and understanding of any situation. Like the depths of the bluest oceans, the calm, still waters of your soul will lead you out of uncertainty to the place of Inner Truth. Always let Insight precede action.

Black
Tourmaline

EMOTIONS

Black Tourmaline

EMOTIONS

Chakra: Root
Color: Black

"I'm afraid of the dark," you cried, as your parents comforted you and turned on a reassuring nightlight. From your youngest conscious moments, you feared that something vile and vicious lurking in that blackness might gobble you up.

The darkness represents the unknown. Fear of the unknown is an accepted human paradigm characterizing the uncomfortable relationship you have with uncertainty. Most of you relate to the unknown as if it were the enemy—a fathomless, unpredictable black hole.

Humans are afraid of the unknown because you assume you have no control over it. What frightens you most is the unknown inside yourself that you may be unable to control. You fear others because their behavior is unpredictable. You recognize too much of yourself in others not to be afraid. What might they do to you, or you to them?

Emotions are the most terrifying aspect of the unknown self for humans. Underneath your carefully manicured and tailored exteriors, you fear there may be a demon waiting to wreak havoc. You correctly sense your unlimited potential. All possibilities imaginable are within you. These options are present so that you can be educated as to what it means to be human. To experience the diversity, humans incarnate many times to attend different schools of experience, much like a field of study in college. Based on what experiences you need for growth, you may decide to be a saint in one life and a murderer in the next.

The purpose of the dark, or anything black, including myself, is to help you delve into undiscovered territory. As a human, your emotions, largely unexplored, are your core. To be fully human, you must investigate each and every one. We assist the Root chakra, the seat of survival and security. Our mutual job is to ground and stabilize you, making it easier for you to balance and work with your emotions.

Emotions are meant to be experienced and contemplated—not condemned. Do not scold yourself for your feelings. Instead, look at the reasons behind your emotional reactions.

For example, when the selfish side of yourself rears its head in a situation, do not chastise yourself for it. Selfishness is engendered by the fear that you will not be provided for adequately. If your life is filled with a poverty consciousness, insecurity would be normal, making it difficult for you to feel generous. Selfishness is what it is, separate from a value judgment. If you feel selfish, you are not a bad person. You are afraid. Do not curse yourself or your emotions.

Different kinds of emotions are frightening to humans. You are particularly afraid of the ones that you label bad, like anger. Who knows what trouble it could get you into? But is anger truly bad? In some situations anger can be your best friend. It can help you protect yourself or someone else.

Humans are almost as afraid of the emotions characterized as good, like happiness. Happiness is a wonderful state. Would you not agree? But you could have another reaction. You may worry that you are undeserving of happiness. Or, you may be fearful that happiness will not last. You may be incapable of enjoying the feeling because of associated negative concerns. In this way, good feelings may become an uncomfortable, unpleasant experience for you.

Emotions, themselves, are neutral, neither good or bad. They are simply teaching tools. They tap into core issues and help you learn through acting out an experience. Emotions are a great gift. Be grateful for them.

Does choosing our card indicate that you have been thinking about your unknown emotional self? What will happen as a result of the emotions you feel or vent? The actions you take because of your emotional condition could be helpful or harmful. When emotions surface, observe them and notice what kind of outcome they generate. With experience, you can make informed decisions about their appropriateness and inappropriateness to create your desired outcomes. Try something different next time if the result is not what you hoped for.

Or might you be concerned about what the future will hold for you? Are you a victim of whatever it decides to bring? The future and the present are not out of your control. You are the creator and the creation. You determine your world by your thoughts, words, and actions. All you need to do is make choices that lead your life on a positive path. If you can shape your future, what is there to fear?

Do not be afraid of the dark. Welcome the unknown in yourself into your heart, for there lie all the possibilities, yet to be created. Their manifestation into matter and reality is up to you. Let all your experiences, all your emotions, be your guide to the ultimate unknown, the Divine.

7

Bloodstone

POTENTIAL

Bloodstone

POTENTIAL

Chakra: Root/Heart
Color: Red/Green

Lifeforce—the fountain of unlimited potential—is sparked when a female and male make love. Technically, you may argue, it is not the act of making love, but the act of sex that creates life. We understand your logic. However, in Truth, the ignition of lifeforce into matter is always generated by Love. Even if the circumstances involving the two personalities seem void of caring or occur in a cruel way.

The Great Creator is always present when a new soul chooses to come into being. This new awakening is the most sacred and love-filled of acts. If you are a parent, look upon your child and see the miracle of beauty and goodness there. Look at yourself and see the same exquisite creation.

Lifeforce is more than pure energy or physical matter. Lifeforce is a spirit-filled essence that exists in every creature. Envision it flowing in every rock, tree, animal, and human on the Planet. It is an essential part of every entity.

If you broke a rock or sawed a tree and red blood oozed from its wounds, you would experience a feeling of kinship. These lifeforms must be like you, you would reason, because they have the same lifeblood. Because you share a commonality, you would probably feel more empathy and respect toward them. We assure you, even though the blood of some creatures is not red, the lifeblood, or Lifeforce, in all of us is the same.

With the activation of Lifeforce that initiated your existence, you were filled with potential. Potential is the unbridled dynamo of possible creativity. When you come into Being, your capacity for ingenuity and resourcefulness is unlimited.

For better or worse, potential is influenced all along the way by external forces. The river's course will leave a town intact or cover it with floodwaters. Rain nourishes the trees or a drought extinguishes their light. In the Human and Animal Kingdoms, your potential is affected by the encouragement or discouragement given you by the significant others in your lives. In recent years, it has also been documented that the Plant Kingdom grows more rapidly with positive reinforcement.

If you have been beaten down, either physically or emotionally, it is critical to neutralize the effects of these negative acts. This is accomplished by understanding that what others have done does not reflect on your worth or your potential. They are simply working out their own melodramas that unfortunately, have involved you.

You are a precious and priceless Universal gemstone. Once you truly believe that, others will lose their power over you. Knowing who you really are, nothing anyone says or does can hurt you because you know the Truth. The recognition of Self can change a life in an instant. Before you were *There,* and now you are *Here. Here* is the center of your being, the wellspring of Potential.

Lifeforce starts your life and keeps you going, but it is so much more than fuel. Throughout your life, it sustains and supports you on emotional and spiritual levels as well. It invests itself in your optimal perpetuation. Why is it so interested in your single existence? Because while you are alive, you have the potential for changing the world through your love and contributions. Lifeforce makes this possible.

Humans have named us Bloodstone because of the red coursing through our green color like blood through veins. The red of the Root chakra produces enlivenment and vitality. The green of the Heart chakra generates love, growth and change. All of these qualities are engendered by Lifeforce so that you may live your life fully.

Picture yourself standing in the back of your mind, looking outward. Ahead of you stretches your entire physical existence. It makes a giant arc in the sky over your head. This arc is composed of Lifeforce. Without Lifeforce, the arc would collapse and there would be no life to view.

The arc is translucent so that you can observe life events acting themselves out throughout its expanse. You can see your past, present, and future all at the same time. You may or may not be able to see clearly what is specifically happening. Remember that the Future is pure potential, changing whenever you do.

Seeing your life literally spread out before you, we hope you will appreciate the investment that the Universe has made in you by bringing you to life. It demands nothing in return. But its great hope is that you will utilize the potential inherent within you. Life is a blessed gift. Why not live it to the fullest?

We mentioned that Lifeforce is not a material substance. But it has a physical representation on the Earth—the sacred fluid: menstrual blood. Monthly bleeding is a signal to men and women everywhere of the potential for new life. And with every new life is the potential for a new World.

In ancient times, the womb was revered as the fertile ground in which a new soul evolves. Pregnancy is a time of preparation for the new being to make its transition from spirit to flesh. When new babies are born, they still remember their time spent on the spiritual plane and their reason for coming into a physical form. The more that they are encouraged while inside the womb by talking, singing, or sending love to them, the easier the transition and the more they will be able to realize their potential.

Why have you drawn the card of Potential today? Are you unsure what your potential is? Are you beginning to investigate in which areas your potential may lie? Or do you already know what you need to be doing, but are not quite there yet? Perhaps you are ready to use your talents, but are looking for the right place.

However you decide to express your gifts, we encourage you to do so thoughtfully, responsibly, and joyfully. The Universe is hoping that you will make the most of your potential for the good of us all. Feel the Lifeforce within you, awakening you to greatness.

8

Boji Stones®

BALANCE

Boji Stones®

BALANCE

Chakra: Root
Color: Golden Brown

All matter is in a state of perpetual motion and evolution. When an earthquake, volcano, or avalanche occurs, the Earth's movement is obvious. Otherwise, it appears to be static. In reality, it is constantly moving, shifting, and breathing.

The Earth's undulation provides us with a mode of transportation. Unusual as it may seem, the Earth propels us forward and we burrow through the earth like a gopher or mole. Our movement is very slow, imperceptible to the human eye. As we move along, we form our bodies by magnetizing particles to ourselves. We push up to the surface of the Earth to complete our formation and fully express ourselves in the form you know as Boji.

Gender identity is not, usually, a characteristic of the Mineral Kingdom. Most minerals combine both the female and male aspects into a single stone. Most Boji stones, however, evolve into a separate female or male self. Each has its own obvious physical attributes. The male has bumpy, geometric protrusions projecting from its ball-shaped body. The female has a smoother, flatter, flying saucer-shaped body.

Our differentiation of gender is not for reproductive purposes. Boji stones do not mate and bear offspring. We evolve differently because of specific tasks that are more effectively accomplished through our separation. One is a unique method of balancing planetary energy fields by working in a grid-like pattern. Another is for balancing emotional states, particularly in the Animal and Human Kingdoms. Occasionally, we assist the Plant Kingdom, as well, if they have experienced extreme trauma.

You, and we, assume female and male forms as part of a mission we are to fulfill. The ultimate goal of the Great Plan is a perfect blending of feminine and masculine energies in every individual. The more often you experience and integrate the best aspects of the two genders within yourself, the more balanced you will be emotionally and spiritually.

Our goal is to help you achieve balance. We work with the Earth as it provides two invaluable services to maintain life. First, it absorbs and neutralizes discordant energies. Second, it replaces them with balanced energy. We usually work unnoticed in the wilderness. But in the last decade or so, humans have taken an interest in us and brought us into their homes and lives.

How can we help you? The most effective way is for you to hold us or our card in your hands. If you have our stone bodies, hold the male Boji in the left, female Boji in the right (if you are left-handed, reverse hands) as you meditate or sit quietly. The two of us function independently, yet synergistically to calm you. Our brown color reflects the energy of the Root chakra. The Root chakra's mission and our own is to help provide balance and stability via our connection to Mother Earth.

We use your vertebral column as an anchoring rod that connects you directly with the grounding energies of the Earth. This extension of yourself travels all the way to the Earth's core.

As you hold us, feel your body fill with space, spread out, and flow into the Earth which surrounds it. The emotions tensing your body and filling your mind are released into the layers of rock and soil around you. Stress, concern, or sadness will leave your body through its outer layers. Once your body is free of these emotions, it can then absorb the nurturance that the Earth so freely offers for healing.

Another way to achieve balance is by going within and tuning into Nature's vibration of harmony. You may not be able to visit a National Forest, a river, or the ocean. You can, however, go out into your own backyard or to a park. Nature is all around you.

Sit on a rock or hold one in your hand or next to your heart. Feel yourself coming into balance under the grounding influence of a mineral. Lean against a tree and feel its energy wash over you and calm you. Find a pond or fountain and experience the songs of the Water Spirits soothing your stressed soul. Sit a little longer, quietly, reverently, and feel yourself merging with your stone, plant, and water kin. You are tapping into the Divine Flow.

Another method of finding balance is through meditation. Once again, the energies of both the Earth and the Universe assist you. Sit quietly with your eyes closed. As you inhale, imagine a stream of light filling each of your chakras as it descends through your body. As you exhale, envision this stream of light travelling deep into the earth. The next time you inhale, breath light into your chakras from the Earth, filling them from the bottom upward. With the exhalation, send this light out into the Universe. Repeat this procedure at least three times.

For the next step, as you inhale, pull light from both the Earth and the Universe into your body simultaneously. Light will fill the chakras from different directions and will exist in your body in parallel channels at the same time. On the exhalation, send Universal Light into the Earth and Earth Light into the Universe, just as you did before. Repeat at least three times. This exercise will balance you on multiple levels and create a feeling of peace and well-being.

Why have you drawn our card today? Is a lack of balance interfering with your work or personal relationships? Balance is difficult in your hectic world. The demands on you are great and stress is ever present. Stress is a destructive vibration, creating anxiety, agitation, and fear. Your physical vehicle cannot endure as much stress as is forced upon you. To avoid illness and injury, you must find your sense of balance.

You are under siege from forces that intend to destroy the natural state of balance of the Earth. These are powerful forces originating from outside the planet, although infiltrating it successfully through your media. This negative energy feeds on itself and multiplies.

It is not our intention to alarm you with this information. But you should be aware that all entities in the Universe do not work for truth and goodness. Some have become destroyers of the Light. There is no reason to fear. Fear exacerbates the problem. The forces of the Light are strong, but we need your help. We urge you to lend your love and light to support this great work.

The Earth needs your balance to balance itself. Center yourself and become one with the Divine Flow. All Nature is there to help you. Pan, the Overseer of the Nature Kingdom, offers his cooperation in helping the Human Kingdom. And so do we. Blessings upon you.

Celestite

GENEROSITY

Celestite

GENEROSITY

Chakra: Throat
Color: Blue

There is no shortage of emptiness in the world—empty pockets, empty jobs, empty marriages. But the most tragic example of emptiness is the empty spirit. An empty spirit may have been drained by hopelessness, loneliness, fear, or resentment. When people feel spiritually impoverished, their tendency is to hold on desperately to what little reserve they have. The remedy for this emptiness is not in hoarding. It is in giving. Even if they feel they have nothing to give, generosity is the medicine they need in order to heal.

Generosity fills the void of an empty spirit as water fills an empty vessel. Generosity is love pouring from one heart into another. It is a response to the cries of distress you hear around you. It is touching another's soul with compassion. Listen with your heart to the hearts of others. They will tell you how you can help.

There are many ways on the physical level that you can share your generosity with others. You might prepare a gift of food. You could donate clothing or contribute to a charity. Offering a warm bed to a friend who is temporarily without shelter is a gift of generosity. You could also volunteer your time to help the homeless, shut-ins, or those with serious illnesses.

We understand that the giving of one's time, help, or home is not always a simple matter. You probably already have more in your life than you can handle—your immediate family, your job, relatives that need special attention, endless meetings to attend, and scheduling nightmares.

You may need to consider practical matters before getting involved. But the true spirit of generosity does not come from the rational, analytical part of yourself. Generosity is spontaneous. It is hearing another's, often unspoken, cry for help and answering in your heart without hesitation. It is an emotional/spiritual connection of empathy from one soul to another. When you feel your heart ache as you see the need in others, respond. Find a way to give of yourself without letting details or inconveniences get in the way of the expression of love.

In your daily comings and goings, you may not pass the homeless on the street, see the loneliness of those in nursing homes, or experience the war-torn lives of those in other parts of the world. You may not immediately recognize that your co-workers. friends, and family have unspoken problems or concerns. With your hectic lives, it is easy to become de-sensitized to your own needs as well as those around you. Look around you. Every day, there are opportunities for giving and helping.

Some humans believe that if you once start giving, there will be no end to it. You will get caught up in the process and become overburdened. This need not be true. If your gift of generosity to others is somehow robbing you of your life or affecting you detrimentally, then you are not being generous enough with yourself. How can you expect to help others if you are not taking care of yourself? As you enjoy saying, "Charity begins at home."

The more you give, the more you receive. Whatever you give

out, you will find returned to you, at least, tenfold. With true generosity, everyone is a winner and no one is a loser. Generosity benefits both the giver and the receiver. And everybody takes turns with these roles. The more freely you can give of yourself, the more of you there is to give.

As you give, look at the intention behind your giving. Whether you give from a compassionate heart or from less than spiritual motives, your gift still may help someone. Then why should it matter? It matters for you. If you are not feeling true generosity toward others, you may have closed off your heart.

If this situation applies to you, give it some attention. Soften your heart to all those in difficulty who touch your life. Many of them may present themselves to you so that you can have an experience with their need and your response to it. Their predicament is a gift to you for your growth.

If you have drawn this card today, look at the issue of generosity in your life. Are you holding back from participating in a cause where you feel you could help? Are you denying the tugging at your heartstrings concerning a friend or family member's dilemma? Are you treating yourself with the care and kindness you deserve?

We are the guardians of generosity between the physical and non-physical spheres. Our name suggests a tie with the Celestial Realm. We also work with the Throat chakra, the center of expression on the Earthly plane. Our blue color is like that of your sky, which you equate with the heavens. We are here to remind you of your connection with the Divine Virtues. These qualities are not only the province of Angelic beings. They are part of who you are, waiting to be expressed.

137

We of the Mineral Kingdom come to help you remember the expansiveness of the human heart. Your heart is not just a contained, physical structure in the middle of your chest. The true essence of your heart is so big that it could swallow the Universe. Do not hold back with your generosity for fear that you will empty yourself and become barren. Your supply of generosity is bottomless and infinite. Give as though all the Universe was yours to give. It is. We stand ready, dear friends, to help you in any way we can.

10

Charoite

COMMITMENT

Charoite

COMMITMENT

Chakra: Third Eye
Color: Purple

Our homeland is near the Charo River in Russia. Hearing that, images flood your mind of what you believe Russia to be. You picture a country whose people are as cold as its climate. You associate Russia with clothing that is drab and outdated, belief systems that are rigid and unyielding, and a government that has permitted few moments of freedom or happiness for its citizenry.

And yet, this country that seems thirty years behind the times is a superpower equalled only by America in the area of nuclear technology, political strategy, and world leadership. Whether its goals are worthwhile or not is not a question we will address here. But Russia has been very successful. What fuels its superiority?

Each country has a collective national personality that affects all of its inhabitants. Russia's vibrational pattern is one of determination, intensity, and relentlessness. This passion of intent is both Russia's greatest strength and its greatest weakness.

The current Russian political revolution opposes the doctrine which everyone once single-mindedly embraced. Instead, now, there are many disparate views that are just as obstinately endorsed, each by its own group of zealots. Warring communities blindly follow their ideals to the death. They are too caught up in unyielding devotion to their particular flavor of nationalism to stop the madness. This is not commitment; this is fanaticism.

Russia's commitment to its principles has made it a great nation. However, unswerving devotion, no matter how well-intended, can often run roughshod over those in its path. Today, Russia is desperately trying to regain its sense of balance.

Russia's crumbling empire offers a metaphorical reminder of what can happen when a country or a person becomes too dogmatic and inflexible. Belief systems are not supposed to be static. They are meant to evolve as change occurs and must be fine-tuned continuously.

Why have we presented this lengthy discourse on Russia? We want you to appreciate that commitment to one's ideals or to a cause can be a noble goal. But like Russia, one can become fixated and single-minded. Do not let your worthwhile intentions cloud your perspective and become your undoing. Balance and flexibility are necessary to achieve and maintain success.

Our message for you also reflects the valuable energy of our homeland. Russia's faithfulness to its beliefs does not exist everywhere in the world. We encourage you to incorporate the energy of commitment into your life. Find something that you feel truly passionate about and devote yourself to it. But unlike our compatriots, approach it with an open and flexible mind.

Do not allow your devotion to a cause to completely overtake your life. Without realizing it, it is possible to become overzealous and move from the position of advocate to fanatic. Being a martyr is a sacred assignment, but one that is unnecessary for most of you to undertake. Most of you will not be called upon to die for your beliefs. Whatever you dedicate yourself to, be sure you enrich the experience and it enriches you. Let your commitment be an important part, but only part, of a rich, diverse existence.

The atmosphere surrounding commitment can be a potentially pious and self-righteous one. People can begin feeling sanctimonious about their important mission. Good intentions, originally born of sincerity, can create a holier-than-thou, *us* and *them* mentality. Russia took itself too seriously. We hope you can avoid making the same mistake.

It is also possible to become confused as to your role in leading others toward the Truth. If you begin seeing yourself as a Saviour, you know you are in trouble. Your involvement is not intended as an ego trip. Leave your personality out of the equation. Maintain a sense of internal balance by remembering your role as an instrument for Universal Love, Light and Guidance. Universal Goodness is working through you. You cannot save the world. But you can help others.

The Third Eye chakra is the center of Inner Knowing. We are its helpmate, bringing our purple energy to help you remember your commitment to yourself and the rest of existence. The Universe offers you encouragement in your practice of dedication. We can help by sending you a lighter, balanced energy of commitment, instead of the heaviness and obsession of extremism. We can also inspire you by reinforcing your natural desire for a better world. We invite you to work with us.

Be sure that along the way you have some fun as you devote your life to meaningful work. Enjoy yourself. As you like to say, "Lighten up." Be serious about your work, but be just as serious about your play. Even with the best of intentions, if you are totally consumed by your work, you will not bring the Highest Good to the project. Balance is the healthy way to approach any project or to live your life.

Why have you drawn the card of commitment today? Do any of the issues we have discussed apply to you? Is it difficult for you to make a commitment? Are you afraid? Examine your life experiences to discover why you feel that way.

Take a look at the commitments you already have. Do you honor them? How much time do you devote to them? Have you either neglected or become obsessed by them? Are you leading a well-balanced life full of meaningful work and fun?

Do you respect others' beliefs even if they differ from yours? Do you ever try to force your beliefs on other people? Do you want to be someone's disciple and follow their guidance? Or do you hope that others will follow you? Explore your relationship with commitment to insure that you are coming from the best possible intentions.

Devote your energy to making the Earth a happier, cleaner, and kinder place to live. Dedicate yourself to the well-being of your fellow Earthmates and your Universal brothers and sisters.

There is much good work to be done. Go inside yourself and ask what is it that you have to offer. Each of us has a special gift waiting to be expressed. Remember to find that place of perfect balance that allows you to contribute your best self and accomplish the most good.

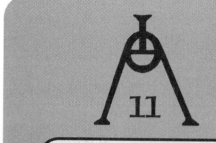

11

Chlorite In Quartz

HEALING

Chlorite In Quartz

HEALING

Chakra: Heart/Crown
Color: Green/Clear

Energy is not just the electrical current that lights your lamps
and runs your appliances. Energy is the multi-faceted facilitator
of healing. It is a consciousness which senses disorder, blockage,
distortion, and separation from the Whole. In humans, these conditions take the form of physical disease, emotional imbalance, or
spiritual distress.

Illness is a sign of obstruction. Divine Energy is designed to
flow through each entity. If there is a blockage of that energy,
imbalance occurs. Often your first realization that something is
wrong is the manifestation of dis-ease on the physical plane. It
might take the form of a tumor, an emotional breakdown, or a
feeling of spiritual isolation.

Your physician may attribute the cause to practical, concrete
explanations—heredity, diet, lifestyle. These may be contribu-
tors, but we assure you that your illness is an outer manifestation of your Inner Self. The origination point for the sickness
will be found farther out on layers of the etheric bodies.

Why do you get sick? People suffer through illnesses for different and, often, complicated reasons. Many dysfunctions of
body, mind, and spirit are caused by unresolved issues surfac-
ing from previous incarnations. These issues may emerge as

feelings of unworthiness, loneliness, rejection, and hopelessness. Your present incarnation is an opportunity for remembering, processing, and releasing these old experiences.

Some of you, when planning your lifetimes on the other planes, decide to take on a medical condition for the good of the Whole. Your illness serves as a context in which others can learn and grow. Through this experience, they may learn forgiveness, unconditional love, compassion, or friendship. You become a teacher for others through sacrifice. Because of your gift, friends and family have an opportunity for understanding and transformation without experiencing the affliction themselves.

Sometimes the purpose of an illness is to destroy a mindset. Many of you believe that some diseases are always fatal—especially AIDS and cancer. Your collective belief system creates a reality where, for many, this becomes the truth. But it can work the opposite way. Individuals who beat the odds and are living healthily often change these predeterminations of death. A message ripples out that death is not the only choice. Hope is reborn.

Frequently, the suffering that humans experience is not due to a physical illness. The unkind words or actions of another, can wound with emotional or spiritual pain that is more intense and more debilitating than any pain of the body. In addition, you might feel distress from dysfunctional patterns and choices in your life. These patterns are clues to unhealed emotional or spiritual areas. Look at what form they take. Certain themes materialize again and again to give you an opportunity to work them out.

The healing process is a complex ritual of energy movement, infusion, and transfusion. When you are being healed, a web of finely spun living cable, only slighter denser than a spider's web enfolds the body. Energy circulates through the cable like blood through veins. It enters the etheric and physical bodies to supply energy as needed to rebalance, cleanse, and heal. Healing occurs on physical, emotional, and spiritual levels.

What is the source of this energy? The Divine Battery that supplies this energy is charged by the collective fusion of individual and group souls. This energy gift is engendered by the compassion and empathy that all creatures feel toward one another. Every entity in the Universe exists to support the joy and well-being of every other being. You are never alone. Others care about you. You always have the help you need.

What health issues caused you to draw our card? Do you need healing in your heart, your body, or your soul? Or does someone close to you? Maybe you are considering a vocation in healing and are exploring its complexities. Perhaps a relationship needs to be healed.

Regardless of the circumstances, willingness is the first step in healing. And courage is the second. Your resolve to face up to a difficult situation or crisis never goes unnoticed or unrewarded. Seen and unseen helpers from all dimensions and all realities rush to your side to lovingly sustain and encourage you.

Never be embarrassed or afraid to ask for help. Asking gives others permission to support you with encouragement or advice. In the process, you will be supporting someone else by providing a chance for them to grow and give. You will get to experience the joy of both receiving and giving. Everyone benefits—an example of a Universal Principle at work. If, by chance, someone you ask for help denies you, be brave and ask another. Even disappointment provides an opportunity for growth.

Your cooperative energy is critical to the Healing Process. You have heard the expression, "God helps those who help themselves." But because this is a Free Will environment, if you do not want to be healed, your decision will be honored. There will be no interference. Every choice you make educates your Soul—and the Souls of all who are touched by your challenges.

Being healed is different than being cured. A person may not survive a physical illness, but may be healed completely. Healing is a function of the Soul. Try not to despair if a loved one's illness seems incurable. It is never too late for healing. Their body may be wasted away, but their heart can still be full and at peace.

Our name is Chlorite. We are a green fountain flowing from the Heart chakra. Our purpose is to heal the spirit. If the heart is closed, no healing can ever take place. Once the heart is open, miracles of healing can occur on all the planes.

We bond ourselves with Clear Quartz for a very special mission. We unite in a marriage of energies to repair, restore, and facilitate the process of health. Quartz is a powerful conductor and amplifier of energy. It works with the Crown chakra, the seat of Universal Consciousness, to intensify the manifestation of healing.

Perfect Health is more than physical well-being. It is a state of Peace and Joy. It is your Divine Right to be healed and healthy. Any other condition is an aberration. Find the Light that heals within you. It will lead you home. May you spend your days upon the Earth in health and happiness. Be well.

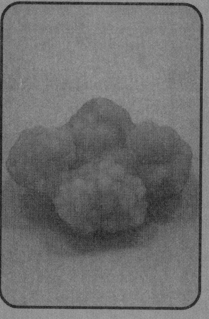

Chrysocolla

COMPASSION

Chrysocolla

COMPASSION

Chakra: Thymus
Color: Blue-Green

Compassion is an outpouring of caring and love that overcomes insensitivity and apathy. Compassion means "to suffer with." When you truly empathize or "suffer with" another, you see that you and they are not so different. As you feel their pain, you set aside your judgments. Through compassion, you begin to recognize the needs of others and feel an urge to reach out to them. When you offer sensitivity, understanding, and reassurance, a connection is formed between your heart and theirs.

An act of compassion between individuals strengthens our overall connectedness, the web that ties all beings together. Indifference toward a ravaged rain forest, a wounded animal, or a blasted mountain tears a hole in the web. It must then be repaired for the Universe to function in proper order. The repair kit is composed of caring, concern, and kindness.

All the Kingdoms must work under a system of mutual respect and cooperation. Chief Seattle understood this when he said that when you affect one being, one species, you affect the whole. There is no division, no hierarchy of worth. No lifeform is superior to another on the planet or in the Universe. This is misinformation. Touch into your rightful place in the Grand Scheme—one of equality with all—human, plant, animal, or mineral.

As you reach out to others, we encourage you to do so, not only physically, but also through your voice. The voice and all sound has much power. Sound is carried on sound waves—a vibration which affects the physical and emotional bodies and has the ability to either soothe and heal—or jangle and disrupt.

The voice carries with it additional qualities other than tone, pitch, or volume. Its emotional component, a special *signature* of love, blesses oneself and others with healing. That is why it is so important to use the voice in a kind, gentle, and responsible way. Choose carefully which words you use and the tone or emotion behind those words. Your heart knows the words that someone else needs to hear. Let it respond instead of your head.

We have heard humans say, " Your words cut me like a knife." In truth, words can cut through the etheric bodies and cause injury. They can particularly damage the emotional self. Occasionally, someone says something which appears to be kind but masks an unkind feeling. Intuitively, you can sense the truth behind the words because their vibration tells the real story.

Why have you drawn the card of compassion today? Do you wish that others would be more empathetic toward you and your life challenges? Do you long for the special caring that compassion brings? Are you opening your heart to others? Have you reached out to someone else in a difficult situation?

In the past, we have worked exclusively with the Throat chakra, the center for communication. Recently, we have entered into an alliance with a new, emerging chakra called the Thymus. It is located between the Throat and the Heart chakras and its color is blue-green, like ours. Our joint purpose is to help you tap into your true self and the resources that reside there.

We offer love and comfort to you. When you feel frazzled or disconnected, we are here to calm and soothe you. Hold our card or our stone body and sit quietly. All the disjointed pieces will shift into harmony, providing a greater understanding of who you truly are.

As you allow your true self to emerge, you will compassionately feel the link between us all. You will recognize yourself as a valuable part of the whole. You will experience the urge to contribute something only you can to make the World more peaceful, joyful, and harmonious. The greatest expression of yourself is in mending the Web of Life with your unique love and gifts.

Reach out, friend, in love, in helping, in the fullness of your heart and your being to all the living entities around you. They need you. They love you. Your compassion is vital to the evolution of the Universe. Let your love wash over all and gentle this troubled world.

13

Clear Quartz

LEADERSHIP

Clear Quartz

LEADERSHIP

Chakra: Crown
Color: Clear

Planet Earth is in need of leaders—people who seek a better world and are not afraid of the challenges that leadership often brings with it. We ask you to give your beauty, light, and talent to the goal of illuminating the world. The way you live your life—your example—will either create a world with more love, or less. Your leadership role in guiding others to a new place of enlightenment is a very important responsibility.

You do not need to be a famous person influencing the masses for your contribution to be worthwhile. You may convince your neighborhood to recycle. You may lead a meditation group for the preservation of the planet. You may pick up trash along a hiking path and inspire others as they see your actions. Everyone has a leadership contribution to make. Simply discover something positive that needs to be done and begin doing it.

As a leader, your behavior becomes a model for others. Be prepared for it to influence your circle of family, friends, and co-workers. Take responsibility for your thoughts, words, and actions. Set the kind of example that you would want to emulate yourself and that would create a better world. The openness of your heart and the quality of your character will set the standard.

The Quartz family is honored to have been selected to lead the Communication Evolution on our planet. Over the last thirty years or so, we have become well-known. The computer industry made us famous when it was discovered that we were an excellent vehicle for the storage of energy and its transportation. Those with a metaphysical orientation made us famous for a different use of energy, that of helping humans open up to their higher consciousness.

These seemingly different fields of study both revolve around communication. The computer communicates information in all the business and service fields around the world. The communication of higher consciousness allows conversations with your Higher Self, all other entities, and the Universe.

In order to open channels of communication to everyone, we have made ourselves easily accessible. Quartz is found everywhere and is usually available for a few dollars. In many parts of the country, you can literally stumble upon pieces of Quartz in the outdoors.

For this time in our history to be a true evolution, as many of you as possible must participate. It is our honor to assist you in opening to your Higher Self. The Higher Self is connected to the Crown chakra with which we work cooperatively. Our clear essence mirrors the energy and intent of this energy center.

We encourage you to work with minerals yourself and give stones to your friends. We would be honored if you chose a piece of Quartz. However, if you feel led to another kind of stone, it may help you or your friend even more.

We can assist you in your desire to open up by suggesting a few methods for working with us. One of the best is to actually wear a Quartz crystal. You may wear it as jewelry, or carry a piece in a pouch or pocket. Not only will your physical energy be elevated, you will more easily establish an open corridor to the Universe and your Higher Self.

Another activity for connecting with Higher Energy is meditation. You can hold one of us in each hand, the point of the right-handed crystal pointing outward, and the left-handed one inward. If you are left-handed, reverse the positions. Working with crystals will deepen and clarify your meditation.

To intensify this experience, surround your chair or meditation cushion with crystals in grid patterns. Some sacred shapes to work with are: the Star of David, the symbol that embodies the phrase, "As Above, So Below," describing our relationship with the Divine; the Circle, symbol of continuity and connection; and the Equilateral Triangle, symbol of balance, tolerance, and equality. Also try the Spiral, the outer point starting directly behind you turning inward in either direction and stopping in front of you. You will need many crystals to physically create the Spiral. As another option, you can envision the Spiral, placing fewer crystals at strategic points in the pattern. Also lay out some of the Crop Circle shapes. You may be able to connect with the messages they communicate.

Leadership in our domain has challenges just as it does in yours. The mantle of leadership is one that we welcomed and accepted. But leadership is not always sought after or appreciated. How are you responding to your role as a leader or to the leaders who affect your life?

In your world filled with emotion, leadership often evokes reactions from others. Some people may want to turn over all their power to their leaders. They follow blindly, assuming everything the leader says or does is without error. Others will be jealous of their leaders' authority and may try to undermine their work. Still others will try to determine if their intention is for the Greater Good and, if so, work cooperatively toward that end.

If you have drawn our card today, you may feel the stresses of leadership issues upon you. They may revolve around an authority figure you are having to deal with or your own leadership position. The responsibilities that accompany leadership often weigh heavily. Viewed from a Universal standpoint, once you elect to undertake an assignment, you make a spiritual pact with yourself. You agree to complete to the best of your ability, whatever needs to be accomplished.

You have powerful leadership ability. Use it for the Highest Good. Many need your sincere and competent direction. Become a leader of the new Millennium. Live your life in a sincere, positive way that others will want to adopt. Your heart is purer than the clearest quartz crystal. We surround you with Light and Love and Friendship.

14

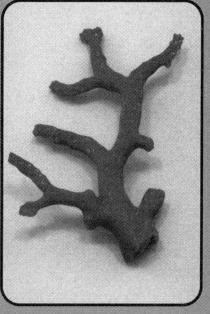

Coral

FELLOWSHIP

Coral

FELLOWSHIP

Chakra: Sacral
Color: Orange

A fellowship is a coming together of souls to share—their support, friendship, love, ideas, common interests, energy, and lives. It is a gathering of Universal Energy designed to unite these souls in communion and community.

Fellowship does not always occur at a planned social event like a party or meeting, although it may. It cannot be orchestrated by calendar scheduling. It often happens over the coffee machine, at a ballgame, or at the grocery store.

Fellowship requires only a willingness to open yourself to another for the sake of establishing a bond of *togetherness.* You may not realize that fellowship is happening until you are well into an interaction. Often, it is not until a conversation has concluded that you realize how magical it was.

How much fellowship are you willing to risk? If you involve yourself with someone, are you afraid of becoming too dependent on them? Humans struggle with the concepts of dependence and independence. Both are valuable traits. It is only in the extreme that either can become undesirable.

Independence allows you to make your own decisions, provide for yourself, and function well alone. Sometimes, though, in an effort to prove that you are completely self-reliant, you can isolate yourself. You may begin to convince yourself that you do not need anyone else.

Other times, you may find it necessary to be dependent on others—for emotional support, physical care, or financial backing. And in those times of need, it is often wise to accept another's help graciously and gratefully. However, dependence taken to extremes can become unhealthy.

The place of balance on the continuum between emotional independence and dependence is fellowship. Neither concept need present a problem. Independence does not mean that you have to go it alone. And dependence does not have to lead to a forfeiting of your power or your individuality. In its truest sense, dependence is the ability to trust——to rely on someone or something else for help or friendship.

Why does our card call to you today? Are you yearning for the love and support of fellowship? Do you want to offer your skills and talents to a group effort? Does the healing of fellowship need to occur within your own family or circle of friends? Do you feel separated from the rest of your global family?

If you are feeling isolated, allow fellowship into your life. You may be attracted to a group whose basis is fellowship. Do the group participants use their strengths and talents for the betterment of the whole? Are all members of this *family* supported in times of joy, accomplishment, disappointment, and grief? Do you experience love, tolerance, and compassion there? If you find this kind of fellowship, participate and enjoy.

You may find the same quality of kinship in a relationship with one person. If fellowship is what you seek, we are not surprised. Many of you long for the intimacy of deep friendship.

Fellowship is not only interacting joyfully with other humans. It is living in harmony and cooperation with all beings. All life is composed of a Common Essence. But because we take on different robes and roles, the connectedness of the Universe is not always apparent.

It is said that if you "walk in another man's shoes," you begin to truly understand who he is. Coral has chosen to do just that by forming a link between two Kingdoms—Animal and Mineral—to comprehend the fellowship that can exist with another species. After the New Millennium, more species will elect to physically merge with other Kingdoms to understand other perspectives by *trying on another's shoes.*

Our merging with another Kingdom is a sign to you of how easily all of us can cross over the boundaries that appear to separate us. All lifeforms are one family. The separation that you perceive is an illusion. Our outer appearances are merely costumes. The challenge is to recognize your friends with their masks on.

You can share an experience of fellowship with the other Kingdoms through the power of your intuition, your openness, and your adventurous spirit. In a meditative state, establish a bridge to transcend the physical so that you can unite with your Plant, Mineral, and Animal kinsfolk. Through this interaction, you will actually experience the physical condition of your planetary brothers and sisters as well as their thoughts and feelings.

Coming together in this way in an environment of peace and allowing strengthens the community we all are part of. The other Kingdoms are always open to making contact with you. We call out to you, but, so far, many of you do not hear us. We encourage you to approach us. Open a space inside your mind and heart where a blending can occur. There is no danger. Believe us, these unions bring much joy.

Coral's work connects you with the Sacral or Second chakra, your center of creativity and sociability. Our orange color represents the spark needed for the germination of a new beginning, as well as the warm feeling of friendship and cooperation that is intended to exist among Kingdoms.

Other lifeforms are like brothers, sisters, or friends to you. Open your hearts to them as you would to a loved friend or family member. If you attempt contact with love in your heart and the intention of fellowship, it will be easy to break through the barriers.

We are your family and we love you. We have come forth at this time to support you and help make your life happier, safer, and easier. We offer our assistance to you in creating a new bond with your fellow inhabitants on the planet.

With mutual trust and caring, together we can create a Family of the Earth that is healthy, supportive, and non-dysfunctional. We urge you to reach out to each other and to the rest of us in love and friendship. Come to our Family Re-Union and join in the fellowship. We welcome your participation and await your arrival with much hope and joy.

Dioptase

COURAGE

Dioptase

COURAGE

Chakra: Heart
Color: Green

Before you can manifest the *courage of your convictions*, you must be sure what your convictions are. If you are confused about your priorities, allow us to help you. It is our privilege to help you go deep into your heart to find what special dream moves you, what sacred belief system guides your life.

Your conscious beliefs and judgments are impressions you have internalized from your environment. Your Soul's true belief system, has developed over the eons of time. Experiences working with Divine Consciousness have helped you create your own internal code of ethics. This code has travelled with you through the corridors of space and time adding new information as you learned and grew.

It is not easy to stand up for and act upon your convictions. There will always be those who will criticize, taunt, and even persecute you for your beliefs. But it is the way of your Soul. Your inner voice is reminding you what is necessary to maintain your integrity—to stay on your path.

Why have you drawn the Dioptase card today? Are you trying to gather the courage to make an important decision in your life? Or perhaps you may be searching for courage to confront someone about an uncomfortable issue. Do you find that each day it takes more and more courage to keep functioning in an unkind world? Why do you especially need courage at this time?

Regardless of your particular issue, we will help you find the courage to *speak your truth and walk your talk*. Courage is within you even though it may be hidden by uncertainty or fear. Together, you and we will travel through fear's shadowy corridors and illuminate them with confidence and hope. Trust us to walk with you and support you in your resolve.

Do you have a choice about whether this is a time to take action or not? You always do. The Great Creator has provided you with Free Will. Whenever you decide to make your journey, we will be here to assist you.

Courage is a gift of the Universe to the Human Kingdom to help you deal with challenges on the Earth plane. The Heart chakra is the translation point for this Universal energy to infuse the physical vehicle. Accept this incredible gift and use it to expand yourself. Look deeply into our green essence and let it activate your spark of courage. Consider it to be your green light for *Go*. You can accomplish whatever you set out to. Your Higher Self, your internal guide, is brave and strong.

Our calm and serene energy is designed to balance you so that your Higher Self can speak and be heard above fear, doubt, and denial. Our soul touches into yours with a gentle, soothing comfort that assures you that you are loved and supported by so many beings in the Universe.

At the same time, we energize and motivate you to take whatever steps are necessary for your Highest Good and for that of the Whole. Stand up for what you believe in and believe in yourself. Your heart will show you the right course.

Your bravery brightens and enhances our World. Your courage to act on behalf of all beings everywhere sets into motion an energy wave that spreads throughout the Universe.

We are all one. We are all connected—the Plants, the Animals, the Minerals, the Humans. All energy is tied together. We are interdependent and responsible for the well-being and health of the Universe.

We honor your work on the Planet. Do your part with a glad and brave heart. Blessings upon you. We are there for you. Do not doubt it.

16

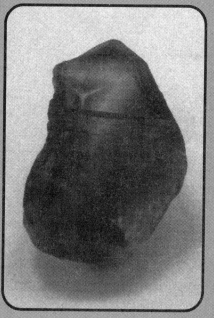

Fluorite

SIMPLICITY

Fluorite

SIMPLICITY

Chakra: Crown
Color: Purple

Envision a desert scene, miles from anywhere. You are surrounded by the spare brush on the desert floor. In the distance you see mesas rising from the Earth and reaching for the sky. Hawks circle, small animals scurry, snakes slither. A peaceful stillness lies over all. This is a place of purity far from the distractions, noise, and confusion of the world you have become so accustomed to. This is a place that knows itself. It does not need a national burger chain for identity. It is comfortable with who it is.

The simplicity of the desert is a symbol of an uncluttered existence. Do you long for a simplification of your demanding life? Freedom from complexity and over-stimulation opens a space within you to entertain some of the profound questions that need to be asked. What is life? Why am I here? How can I help? Is there more to my existence than this everyday hum-drum? If so, how can I get in touch with it? Where is the room in your busy schedule for asking these questions or receiving any answers?

Perhaps the issue of whether these questions need to be asked and answered has not arisen in your life. But you may wonder why you often feel an emptiness and longing. To fill this void, you may try food or shopping trips to the mall. But, unfortunately, material goods do not satisfy your need. The dress you buy may hang in your closet for months before you wear it. The fishing tackle may stay unused even longer.

The fulfilled feeling you search for can only be found by stripping away the extraneous from your life. Then the true essence of your existence will be revealed. Does this mean that you need to become a monk or a nun? Not unless you feel a calling for those vocations. Are we suggesting that you throw out all your belongings and reject material goods? That could be unrealistic.

It is essential, though, to disentangle yourself from the chaos that surrounds you and all that feeds it. The frenzy of your day-to-day lives is pervasive. You cannot escape it unless you make a conscious effort.

Have you chosen our card today because you want to return to a more basic life? Do you feel a need to re-prioritize what is truly important and essential? Would you like to replace savoir-faire and sophistication in your interactions with purity and integrity? Do you dream of a return to innocence?

Your desire is the first step from which a new lifestyle can grow. A next step might be to sit down and make two lists side by side. One would contain the fundamentals you consider necessary for a fulfilled life. The other would include your current life activities and possessions. Does your life today support the lifeplan you would like to build for tomorrow? If the two lists are at odds with each other, consider how you can bring them into harmony. Make adjustments in your life based on what your heart tells you.

Acknowledge the psychological over-crowding that you are forcing yourself to endure. This is a pollution of your spirit, for which a decontamination may be required. To move from your jam-packed existence to one of simplicity, free yourself from the unfulfilling patterns that hold you back.

The Crown chakra is the place where ultimate simplicity and ultimate complexity co-exist. This chakra holds Universal wisdom to be used in physical incarnation—the ability to distill the many truths into The Truth. Fluorite's purple energy assists the Crown chakra by helping you see the larger picture beyond the clutter of your daily existence.

A return to simplicity may require getting into a different environment to break the spell of the siren's call to routine, production, and competition. A place of solitude would provide a conducive environment where you could quietly and mindfully face yourself and your life questions.

If this is impossible at this time, take time every day to meditate or find a quiet place out in Nature to relax and think. Some people touch into that stillness while running or exercising. Discover where it is that you can quiet and center yourself to do your important inner work.

A washing away of worldly concerns, fascinations, and preoccupations will clear your mind and spirit to receive. Simplify your life. Purge yourself of the addiction to the fast lane and all its baggage. Step off that express train to nowhere. Let your spiritual destination be the unspoiled and serene environment of the desert. Simplicity is the path to awareness and fulfillment waiting for you there.

17

Golden Calcite

POWER

Golden Calcite

POWER

Chakra: Solar Plexus
Color: Gold

Within each one of you is a reservoir of power, a golden orb, in the center of your being. In the physical body, it is located at the Solar Plexus area, above your navel. Your Higher Self moves plans and ideas into this Third chakra for empowerment. The Solar Plexus operates like an engine to fuel your intent and bring your goals into manifestation.

The Solar Plexus works in your physical body like the Sun works in the Solar System. It provides the necessary energy and warmth for your inner crops to grow and bear fruit. It is an energy vortex, a dynamo, that drives your will.

Willpower is not a forceful, aggressive expression. If fact, no force at all is necessary to invoke the power of the will. When you engage your willpower, you tap into a mature reserve of confidence. There is no foot stomping, no tantrum throwing. There is resolve and stability.

Not only do you generate your own power, but we blend our golden energy with the Solar Plexus to gather power for you from other energy sources. For instance, Nature, in all her abundance, is a constant supplier of power. The other Kingdoms also freely offer to merge their energy with you.

Some people seek to overpower others for selfish reasons. They believe that by gaining control over another they can take their power for themselves. They will be disappointed. Power that is stolen will not work for the benefit of the thief.

Many of you may recall a past lifetime when you remember misusing your power. You may have been a powerful person as society defines it. You had many possessions and much wealth. Others were afraid of you. You may have literally held their life in your hands. Trust us, this is not power. This is subjugation and domination.

True power is not gained through intimidation, dirty tricks, or stepping over someone else to get what you want. True power comes from knowing who you are, what you want, and determining a way to get it without injuring anyone else along the way.

Let this be your guide. Ask that whatever it is you want be accomplished only if it is for the Highest Good of all beings everywhere. Then you will know, with certainty, that if it comes to pass, it will be a blessing for all.

You can invoke your power for good or for ill. Just as your thoughts create your reality, your Will creates outcomes. You are still the Wizard of ancient times. Spiritual Sorcery uses Good to effect change. Observe its potency as you see the power of love transform someone's life. Wizard, you are wise. Do not use any distorted motives to create negativity. Use your power to heal and help, instead of hurting.

Power is a huge issue on the planet and has been since the beginning of time. If you have drawn this card today, you may be having difficulty with a power struggle in your life. It may be over control of your children. It might be in a romantic relationship. It could be work-related.

Human societies are obsessed with being Number One. Your world is based on competition. Many humans get ahead by pushing others behind. The Universe functions on cooperation, where every being benefits. The frenzy to be in control of others and the discordant emotions which accompany it, are at the heart of the chaos in your world.

Change your world by using your power to unite, rather than to conquer or divide. Listen to your saying, "It matters not who wins or loses, it's how you play the game."

Invoke your gentle, kind, and strong will to heal yourself, your relationships, and our planet. We watch and wait and are with you through it all. We cradle you in the golden light of our love.

18

Green
Tourmaline

Abundance

Green Tourmaline

ABUNDANCE

Chakra: Heart
Color: Green

Scarcity is an illusion. Abundance is a reality. There is always enough of whatever you need. Unfortunately, fear has made you believe otherwise.

Over the millennia, there have been entities who have manipulated your emotional state to their advantage. Because they want to remain in control, they generate fear-based scenarios that keep you preoccupied. If you are worrying about whether or not you will have the money to buy food or clothes, you will not have time to remember your true self and your inheritance.

Your birthright as a child of Mother Earth is abundance. This may seem hard to believe as you observe the obvious poverty of homeless people on the streets. This *reality drama*, among others, has been created by unfriendly forces as a means to elicit detrimental emotional responses in humans.

Use the plight of the homeless as an example of a disheartening condition on the planet. What are some of the possible reactions you might have to their misfortune? You might respond with compassion and decide to help the homeless. You might respond with disgust, thinking that they brought it upon themselves. You might be indifferent, not giving them your attention at all.

The way that most of you respond is with fear—that it could happen to you. These situations are designed to disturb you because they represent a mirror of the possible. Getting the reaction that they want, the beings who orchestrate these emotional melodramas expose you constantly to this image or others like it that generate fear. They use your fear as a tool to keep you immobilized, vulnerable, and powerless.

Our job as emissaries of the Mineral Kingdom is to help you remember that you need not be afraid. Everything you need is available to you—waiting for you to claim it. You have unlimited credit on your Universal Abundance Card. Not just for money and material possessions. The true gifts of abundance are those of the Spirit—Love, Peace, Joy, Faith. With these assets, everything else automatically follows.

You have been programmed to believe just the opposite. If you can replace your fear with confidence that abundance is everywhere, there will be one fewer human to perpetuate the lie of scarcity. When you withdraw your energy from the fear side and move it to the faith side, an energy shift occurs.

You may not think that a change in one person could make much difference. You are mistaken. Your emotional and spiritual contribution affects the collective unconscious like a dark cloud opening and exposing the Sun. Your change in perspective is an energy wave that spreads across the Universe carrying the power of Light and Love. The paradigm of fear is weakened significantly by your departure—like a house whose structure is compromised by the removal of a brick. Eventually, as others release their fear and move into faith, the house of fear will topple.

How do you move from a poverty consciousness to a prosperity consciousness? First, turn your focus away from the world of manmade things and look around you at the natural world. Nature sends a message of abundance, season after season, in the renewal of the sprouting plant and the leafing tree. Even if a drought or forest fire appears to devastate an area, there will be growth again. If, in your life, there are seasons when you are in need, trust that like the tenacity of Nature, your inner determination will help you survive and thrive once more.

Do you have a concern over abundance that has caused you to draw our card? Sometimes life hands you challenges that seem unbearable. Circumstances make you feel as though you are financially, emotionally, or spiritually bankrupt. In these times, you must be a keen observer to see the prosperity in your life.

Try looking beyond the obvious dilemma at what you *do* have, instead of what you *do not*. Obvious assets tend to be overlooked in times of crisis. You may have forgotten resources which this adversity will bring to light—friends, family, your own inner strength and courage, the company of Angels to journey with you. If the blessings of your life still seem obscured, look farther and see that the whole of the Universe is offering you friendship and support.

The cycles of Life teach you about appreciation. Even when appearances are to the contrary, opportunities for good fortune reside in all experiences. There are always valuable lessons to be learned. Expect a blessing in every situation.

Let us help you when you are disheartened or worried. Hold us or our card in your hand. Feel your shoulders relax, your pulse slow down, your breathing deepen. Feel your spirit fill with reassurance that you are well provided for. We shower you with the essence of abundance. We are the Heart chakra's ally, quieting your anxiety, helping you open and embrace everything with love. Fear cannot live where love abides.

Although you may not realize it, what you fear most is the poverty of spirit—losing your connection with the Divine. You are the Universe's sweet child. It will not desert you. You are forever in its embrace.

Remember an important Universal Principle: the prosperity that you encounter will be effected by your willingness to accept the good that is flowing into your life. This acceptance is predicated on feeling worthy of receiving such a blessing.

Green is the color of growth, abundance, generosity, health, and love. All of us are defined in part by the colors we carry. Learn the significance of color and you will be able to read the messages that are posted for you everywhere.

Our color communicates the abundance of Nature, always renewing and replenishing itself and all in its dominion. Paper money is green, a symbol from your forefathers of the prosperity your currency holds. Everything green is a reminder of the abundance that surrounds you.

Abundance may not always come as you expect it. The Universe is full of surprises. Be assured that whatever form it takes it will bring wealth to your life. Look for the silver lining in all experiences. There are treasure chests continuously opening for you.

Do not worry that you will be empty-handed. Make sure that you are not empty-hearted. Abundance means fullness. If your heart is full, your life will be also. We love you, dear ones.

19

Hematite

NEUTRALITY

Hematite

NEUTRALITY

Chakra: Root
Color: Charcoal Gray

"Is it black or white?" you ask. "It is neither," we answer. It is gray. And so are we. The world of humans is one of polarity—of extremes. Everything is measured—black or white, good or bad, innocent or guilty, right or wrong. In truth, the Universe is a gradation of grays. On your planet those who work in the field of photography call it the gray scale—shades of gray ranging from pure white to pure black.

When you give this issue of opposites your attention, you will see that what might appear to be a certain way in one circumstance may seem just the reverse in another. For instance, the act of theft. Is it wrong to steal something from another that does not belong to you? You may answer without hesitation, "Yes." But what if a mother steals bread to feed her children? Perhaps she has done everything she can to get work and to be a responsible parent, but she has come to her last resort, theft. What then?

The Universe is made up of indefinites. We have told you that at any moment you can change, circumstances can change, life as we know it can change. The dynamism of the Universe is built upon the radical possibilities that infinite change offers.

Quantum physics has altered the scientific community's mind about the, once, indisputable laws proposed by well-known physicists.

Acts occur randomly. And yet even within that randomness there is a plan, an order, an organization of form and function.

Our message to you is one of neutrality. The Root chakra is the channel through which all emotionality, negativity, and bias is channelled into the Earth to be neutralized. This neutralization returns energy to the surface for use in an untainted form.

Neutrality is impartial, implying a willingness to see many possibilities. It encourages not looking for the only answer, but for the best answer. The heart of neutrality is to remain unbiased and open—to consider all the evidence upon which to make a decision.

On occasion, to remain neutral, one must suspend judgment or decision-making. This can be a very uncomfortable predicament. Many of you feel better forming an allegiance to one side or another, *choosing up sides*. This need for life to be neatly ordered and defined, is driven by the polarity and duality of your physical incarnations on Earth.

The urge to rally round a cause, a doctrine, or a system accounts for much of the separatism in your world. Everyday, decisions about a person's or product's worth are based on arbitrary measurements that are often without merit.

If you have drawn this card today, perhaps you have made a judgment or decision about someone or something that needs rethinking. Chances are, the truth about the situation may fall more into the gray scale than into a totally black or white extreme. Taking the time to look in an unbiased way may allow new insight and clarity.

Maybe it is you that has fallen under severe scrutiny. Have you done it to yourself or has someone else judged you unfairly? If you have treated yourself unkindly, then here is an opportunity to practice more tolerance. If others have done it to you, what better chance for the mirror to reflect the severe judgment which you might, potentially, inflict upon another.

Neutrality needs a non-condemning heart to function. The closed heart and the already convinced mind allow no room for change, forgiveness, or redemption. If it is your desire to call all beings everywhere your sister and brother, it will be necessary to sacrifice your need for pigeonholing everything around you. The act of classifying and categorizing, in itself, isolates you.

To hold some opinion with absolute certainty requires a lot of energy. It requires a stiff neck, a rigid back, a tension that does not allow being in the Divine Flow of the Universe. When your heart, instead of your head, reveals to you the Truth surrounding an issue, your body, mind, and spirit relax. This physical awareness of ease is a sign to you that you are not forcing your will or your set of standards on the rest of the world.

Maintain the neutrality that unconditional love offers. Love creates a circle that encompasses, not excludes. Forgiveness provides a place where old perceptions are forgotten, given up for a lighter heart.

Reconsider all the clearly defined beliefs you have established to keep your world an ordered, safe environment. You will find that, other than to provide structure, many may have questionable value. Trade the useless ones in and relax into a neutral position. Entertain the possibilities open to you. Experience what it feels like to float freely without the constrictions and restrictions that definitive judgments place upon you.

Whenever you see the gray of our bodies, remember how liberating it can be to look beyond the extremes—to be open-minded and open-hearted. Bless you in your journey. All of us support you.

20

Kunzite

ENTHUSIASM

Kunzite

ENTHUSIASM

Chakra: Heart
Color: Pink

Enthusiasm is excitement about the potential of life—an eagerness to discover what life has to offer and an urge to get involved. The people of France have the perfect expression for enthusiasm—*joie de vivre*—joy of living. When you are joyful about life, everything you do is infused with enthusiasm.

Enthusiasm brings a quality of sacredness to your work or any endeavor. Because of your enthusiasm, you open a portal into which the Universe can pour its cooperative energy and power into your project. What a valuable gift enthusiasm offers to the world!

Your expression, *getting turned on,* beautifully illustrates the feeling of enthusiasm. When you are enthusiastic, you feel alive, as though your system had actually been switched on. In truth, your body shifts into a different bio-electrical state.

The outpouring of enthusiasm from your open Heart chakra activates endorphins in your system that make you feel exhilarated and happy. Neurotransmitters in the brain begin circling energy in the body at an accelerated rate.

The next time you feel really enthusiastic about something, notice your physical reactions—an increased heart rate, warmer skin temperature, and a tingling along the spine. You have been *enlivened*—filled with life—by the potential of an idea, a relation-ship, your work, or your existence.

But what about times that you do not feel so enthusiastic? You may be motivated to do something out of necessity, but not really be enthusiastic about it—like completing an assignment because you have a deadline, cleaning your house for guests, or cooking dinner because you are hungry.

Make an effort to approach tasks you would like to avoid with a positive and enthusiastic attitude. Motivation driven by negativity will not yield the Highest Good. Without enthusiasm, you rob yourself of a potentially joyful experience and the overall quality of whatever you accomplish will be affected. Eliminate any unnecessary emotional baggage from your project that might come between you and your success.

Our job with the Heart chakra is to help you get in touch with the feeling of enthusiasm. We would like to paint a picture that you may relate to emotionally. Imagine lying back on cool grass, waiting for and then watching firecrackers explode against a dark sky on the Fourth of July. Remember the feeling of hopeful-ness, excitement, and exhilaration that you experienced.

Permit us to help you tap into that exuberant feeling so that you can access it whenever you need it. Sit quietly and meditate with our pink stone body or our card. Sense the physical changes occur as you allow a ripple of enthusiasm to flow throughout your body and positive images to fill your mind. Notice your elevated spirits and emotional lightness.

Anticipation is a natural companion to enthusiasm. Anticipation implies faith in the unseen future to produce a miracle. Looking forward to your next new relationship, job, or adventure invites the Universe to fill your life with a wealth of rich experiences.

Enthusiastic people are often open to a range of possibilities, allowing for unexpected good fortune. There are no guarantees when you set off enthusiastically in any new direction. You may think you know what lies down the road, but what really happens is often a surprise. If you greet new experiences with anticipation and enthusiasm, rather than fear, life can be an adventure. And the Unknown will be a friend rather than an enemy.

Enthusiasm also breeds spontaneity. Go ahead—give in to this deliciously bold feeling. Occasionally, do something without analyzing every step. We are not advocating reckless behavior. But we encourage you to move forward unreluctantly, without coercion from others, and without restraining yourself unnecessarily. Doing so can help you free up a lot of creative energy that you may have been holding back.

Spontaneity helps create, within you, a place of anticipation into which the Universe can pour your possible futures. If there is no room prepared for these experiences, they cannot take up residence. Then you will have to go searching for your good fortune, instead of it presenting itself to you.

Why have you drawn our card today? Are you missing liveliness in your life? Does your daily existence seem more like drudgery than delight? Do you have projects to complete that are weighing you down? Try to remind yourself each morning upon arising that the day will be much happier and easier, if you tap into the natural energy of enthusiasm. Enthusiasm can infuse your day with vitality, self-determination, and fun.

Discover how you can bring enthusiasm into your life. Get excited. See how invigorating it feels.The positive effects of the passion, curiosity, and imagination that are part of enthusiasm create a zest for life. Whenever you begin feeling down, remember your last experience with enthusiasm.

Perhaps you are already enthusiastic, but have not found the proper vehicle to which to lend your enthusiasm. You may be searching for the right project or calling. Or, if you already have a project in mind and others are unresponsive to your dreams, try not to let them squelch your enthusiasm.

Enthusiasm is an elixir for animating your spirit and your life. Allow its power to lead you to the next exciting adventure. Bless you on your journeys.

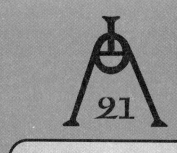

21

Kyanite

HAPPINESS

Kyanite

HAPPINESS

Chakra: Throat
Color: Blue

Surrender to happiness. This is the message we share with you. We encourage you to fill yourself and your life with the liquid of pure joy. Release any hesitations you may have about experiencing the elation of life's happy moments.

Happiness is a special compensation of your Earthly sojourn. Your ultimate goal here is enlightenment and reunion with the Divine. But before you get to that point, and while you are in the physical body, happiness lights up your life.

Unfortunately, your world is pessimistic about the possibility of happiness. Someone is always cautioning you about getting your hopes up. With good reason, many of you are hesitant. You have been disappointed when you counted on someone for happiness.

Many of you have decided that the safest route is not to entertain any expectations. You will have a shorter distance to fall, you reason, if you do not build yourself up. If you do not allow yourself to hope, you may not experience as much pain if something goes wrong. But neither will you experience the joy. When life has so much possible happiness to offer, is this the way you want to live your life?

Reluctance gets in the way of many of the blessings of your physical existence. Hesitation and doubt cripple your enjoyment of life. Most of the awful things that you imagine may happen, never come to pass. In the meanwhile, fear may cause you to miss out on the beauty of a once-in-a-lifetime event.

The experience of happiness is felt physically, emotionally, and spiritually. It is an overflowing of exuberance which cannot be contained by the physical vehicle. It must express itself in your posture, facial expression, tone of voice, and the words that you speak. It prompts you to reach out to others and by proximity they are affected by your joy. Happiness is a manifestation of your Divine Self.

We want to assist you in touching into this well of joy within you. Kyanite works with the Throat chakra, the center of expression. Our mutual goal is to help you recognize and express your true self so that joy may be your constant companion. Our blue color is a vehicle for the expression of happiness through its greatest medium, your life.

Why has Kyanite's card appeared for you today? Is your life filled with joy? If not, look around you with new eyes to see the beauty and wonder of your world and the many blessings in your life. Are there any questions in your mind about whether you deserve to be happy? Let us assure you; you are profoundly worthy of happiness. Happiness is part of who you are, an essential element of your DNA programming.

This is the truth. But we can not force it upon you. You know from experience that when others say nice things to or about you, you may disregard their compliments. Your perception of yourself and their impression of you may not always agree.

Many of you see only the flaws in yourself and not the beautiful character traits and talents. If this is the case, others may see you more clearly than you do yourself.

We want to pay you some of the biggest compliments you have ever had. You need not be suspicious of us. We have no ulterior motives. The only thing we want from you is that you recognize the exquisite creation that you are, totally deserving of joy.

You are the beautiful and beloved daughters and sons of Mother Earth. The Universe treasures you as a glorious and shining star. You are cherished by your own private support group of Angels and Guides waiting to assist you. We would not deceive you. As you read these words, feel your heart open and allow the truth to convince you.

You have unexpected bliss ready to enter your life. It is waiting for you as love, money, success, a new baby, or the job you have always wanted. Good fortune is abundant everywhere in the Universe. It is attracted like a magnet to those who believe that being JOY-FUL is the natural state.

Will you give happiness a try? What have you got to lose? And what might you have to gain? If you are still unsure about the risks involved, reread our message and take a chance.

Envision happiness as a big pool. Go ahead. Dive in. Do not worry about whether it is deep enough. It is bottomless. The most sincere way of thanking the Universe for this amazing gift is by immersing yourself in it. Put aside your doubts and embrace as much happiness as you can. Be what you were meant to be—blissfully happy.

22

Labradorite

AUTHENTICITY

Labradorite

AUTHENTICITY

Chakra: Thymus
Color: Blue

Who are you? When asked this question, most of you describe yourself by either your gender, a role you play, or your profession. "I'm a woman." "I'm a mother." "I'm a computer programmer."

Do you have an identity that transcends your relationships to others? Who are you beyond these limited parameters? If you want to know more, how can you find out? Self-discovery holds the answers to your individuality. Learning how you came to be who you are is critical to a happy, productive life.

Countless numbers of you have resolved to revisit and deal with unfinished business from your past. The reason? To recover lost fragments of your lives without which you cannot be whole.

Why were these life experiences left behind? Some may have been too painful to remember. Whether you experienced serious abuse or simply the thoughtless insensitivities of others, all of you have been wounded sometime in your life. As a protective device, your mind locked away incidents that were too debilitating to live with. Consequently, you have been denied access to valuable information that has shaped who you are.

Emotional patterns and belief systems establish themselves early on. Significant events of the past hold the key to your emotional make-up, your behavior, and your motivations.

As you observe yourself, you may notice that you routinely react to certain stimuli in a particular way. The reason for your reaction may be a mystery. Rediscovering your personal history can unlock the past—helping you recognize and change dysfunctional, unproductive behavior and resolve old, emotional issues.

It takes great courage to face the memories of an emotional or physical trauma from the past. Your search for authenticity involves devoting the time, energy, and emotion necessary to confront the truth. It also demonstrates the respect you have for yourself. Once aware of the dynamics that influenced your development, you can work through and release them. You are not a prisoner of your past. Self-knowledge can set you free.

Become self-conscious. You heard us; we said self-conscious. Unfortunately, this phrase has taken on the negative meaning of being uncomfortable with yourself. In truth, self-consciousness provides the ultimate comfort. Authenticity brings peace. But how can you determine whether you are being authentic without, first, being self-aware?

Currently, a phenomenon in human evolution is awakening a new chakra in the physical body. This emerging chakra is located between the Throat and Heart chakras, at the Thymus. The catalyst for this physical manifestation is the spiritual breakthrough of the reclaiming of Self. Our blue color and energy are linked with the Thymus chakra that is materializing. We are honored to be part of this new development in human history.

Why have you selected our card today? Have you been yearning to understand yourself better? The arrival of this new chakra symbolizes a reacquaintance with yourself. Perhaps you have been unconsciously pretending you are someone you are not. Authenticity eliminates the need for deception.

The image you present to the world is, in part, comprised of acted-out expectations from your family, friends, and other important people in your life. As you begin to rediscover yourself, you may find that you are not who you think you are. You may have lost part of yourself trying to be someone else for others.

Life changes. People come and go. You and your significant other may part ways. Your children will grow up and move out. The only constancy in your life is that you will always be there. Build a personal identity for yourself that makes *you* happy—one based on authenticity and self-respect.

The ancients said, "Know thyself." This guidance is as valuable today as it was long ago. Use all the tools available to find out who you are. Self-awareness is a starting point to reach the goal of self-realization. You can not realize what you do not recognize.

Uncovering and dissecting all those old, buried memories is the hardest part of the process. Creating a new, authentic life is easier. Eliminate anything that does not contribute to your abundance, joy, and peace. It sounds simplistic, because it is. You are the Universe's bright star of hope. We applaud your integrity.

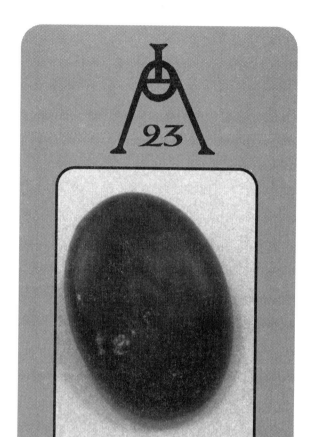

Lapís Lazulí

MAGIC

Lapis Lazuli

MAGIC

Chakra: Third Eye
Color: Dark Blue

The world of magic is the world of illusion. As you say, "Now you see it, now you don't." The mysterious, the mystical world, surrounds you. You cannot always see its inhabitants, because there is a veil that separates you. When you meditate, you often penetrate this veil.

All occurrences that are attributed to magic have explanations—for example, the act of invisibility. It is not as mysterious as it seems. A person can disappear by introducing so much space in between his molecules that he cannot be seen and recognized as his former self. Another way to become invisible is to simply walk into another reality. You have not truly dematerialized, but your frequency has shifted. You may realize that you know some of these tricks, but they lie dormant within you.

Why do we tell you these magical secrets? Because we want you to know that you are a magician yourself. You can change the reality you inhabit into a different one anytime you like. The tool of magic provides a sustaining confidence that anything is possible. And if you believe that anything is possible, there is no cause for depression, doubt, or concern in your life.

The way of magic is multi-fold. Magic allows for unnatural occurrences to happen, so that the Universe can introduce unexpected wonder into your life that you might not project for yourself. It also puts into your control the manipulation of events to your advantage. You have a saying, "Be careful what you wish for, you might get it." The reason that this saying has become so popular is because on a higher level you recognize that it is true.

As with all things, you have a choice about how you will use the magic available to you. There have been many throughout the ages that have misused the power of magic. We encourage you to be responsible for your actions. No harm should be done to any creature in the service of your own needs. If you use magic for the detriment of others, you may lose your power and add karmic debts to your account.

The ways of magic have, for the most part, been lost to humankind. Now that many of you recognize that you can create your own reality, magic is returning. As yet, you have no idea how much control you have over this gift.

Some of you are just beginning to use your magical talents again. You get excited when you envision a parking space and one becomes available. This is a great reinforcement of what you can accomplish magically. But while you are locating a place to park, also consider trying to bring about world peace. At this stage of your career as a magician, some of you feel confident enough to create small magic in your life, but you do not yet have the confidence to create a miracle.

You have made a good start. Parking spaces let you know the magic is working. Trust us, we do not demean your efforts. We simply want to encourage you to believe in yourself and your abilities—the real magic.

To make your life whatever you want it to be, you must believe that you can. Nothing is impossible—unless you believe that it is. Since nothing is impossible, the possibilities are endless.

If you have drawn this card today, you may be feeling that you want more magic in your life. You may wish you could say a few abracadabras and conjure up a new reality. If so, intend that the most delightful experiences will happen. At first, leave your intentions open-ended and let the Universe convince you of the variety of ways magic can express itself. Later, when you are feeling more confident, try intending that something specific occur. Use the power of your words, spoken aloud and in your mind, to declare that magic is going to occur.

Magic brings a sense of excitement and joy. There is much happiness in knowing that a world of possibilities is open to you. The more you believe in yourself and your magical ability to change your present and your future, the easier it will become. Your confidence will create more and more magical events in your life.

To generate magic in your life, believe that the unbelievable can happen. Whether it is in yourself, your abilities, or the reality of peace, belief in anything brings power to it.

In ancient times, we were the Wizard's companion and help-mate. A number of us from the Mineral Kingdom agreed to accept as our work the first communications with humans. Lapis Lazuli took on as our role assisting humans in performing the magic that was, then, an everyday affair. The Third Eye chakra is the place of magic and shape shifting. We facilitate its mission and operate on the same dark blue frequency.

Tragically, over time, humans forgot that it was they who were creating the magic and that we were only assisting. They began to doubt their abilities and turned to us as the source of their magic. We are communicating today to remind you that YOU hold the magic.

In those days, shape shifting was common. Today, as in olden times, you have the ability to shift your body, your work, your relationships, and your world. You were not meant to lead a life of boredom or drudgery. You have a higher purpose that you have chosen for yourself. You are built for greatness. Each one of you has a special destiny to fulfill.

We are always excited to come into contact with the Human Kingdom. Join us on a great adventure. We will travel to places you have never even dreamed of, let alone been to. We will be your guide and your protector into the world of the impossible made possible.

Magic is creativity and vice-versa. Let magic help you give birth to the beautiful life you deserve. Imagine what you want and then say the magic word. Godspeed.

24

Larimar

FREEDOM

Larimar

FREEDOM

Chakra: Throat
Color: Blue

Imagine looking out onto a golden dawn. Picture yourself as an energetic youth climbing to the top of a mountain. Upon reaching the summit, you look into the face of the Sun. You spread your arms and fly. As you float gently above the Earth, a beautiful song flows from your being.

You sing from every part of yourself. You sing from a place so deep that although it comes from within you, it originates far beyond you. The song you sing is for the liberation of all creatures. As this vibration reaches them, it fills their hearts and frees their souls.

Not everyone will have the talent of a great singer, but your voice can be even more powerful as a vehicle for freedom. Freedom of Speech is a guarantee of the American tenets of Democracy. Use your words to encourage others to unlock the feelings of fear, anger, guilt, shame, and hate that imprison them. Releasing these restricting emotions will free up spaces that can ultimately be filled with confidence, love, self-worth, and peace.

Imprisonment can take many forms. The type of prison that one experiences may range from true incarceration to the paralysis of fear. Most *dramas of confinement* will act themselves out in a familiar venue. Your jail might be a marriage you feel trapped in, a job that you hate, or the responsibility of caring for an elderly or ailing family member.

Freedom is a decision. No person or circumstance can tie up your soul unless you allow it to happen. If you submit, you become an accessory to the crime. The shackles that you wear may have been placed there by another, but only you can remove them. No one else has the key to your prison. Freedom is not the unlocking of a cell door, it is the unlocking of the spirit.

Challenging circumstances occur for your growth. Your Higher Self orchestrates situations in which you can test yourself to see what buttons get pushed, and how you respond. The way you deal with your predicament will cause one of two things to occur. The experience will either set you free to fully love and learn from what has happened or it will chain you to guilt and resentment. How you approach and come to terms with these life challenges will determine the outcome.

Planet Earth is a free-will environment. The Free-Will Zone is a structure through which you can learn about the consequences of your actions. Think about any challenging situation you have faced. You have always come out wiser as a result of the experience.

Since you are free to learn in any way you want, we encourage you to choose joyful experiences for yourself. Make up your mind that all your life lessons will be positive and life-affirming and that you will learn them easily and effortlessly.

We repeat what others have said—you do not need to learn through pain or misfortune. You have been programmed to believe that deservedness must be earned and that life is hard. This is misinformation. Just the opposite is true.

As a spark of Universal Energy, the freedom that you enjoy allows for unlimited Good in your life. Only your belief system gets in the way of your receiving it. Eliminate the roadblocks and see how effortless your journey becomes.

Is there someone or something in your life that you are desperately afraid of losing? If so, your fear may be imprisoning you. Fearful attachments to material possessions, relationships, and jobs create feelings of loss and lack. These emotions lead to territoriality, paranoia, and distrust. You and your attachments are cell mates chained to each other. Escape this bondage. Fear blocks the flow of joy and prosperity.

Allow us to help you in your quest for freedom. When you see our coloration, let it remind you of the blue sky. The sky is the domain of Air, in which you, too, can be "free as a bird." Open your cage; sing out for freedom; spread your wings and fly. You no longer have to be a prisoner. The freedom of your spirit has no boundaries or limitations.

We work with the the Throat chakra, the center of expression. Our blue color lends power and inspiration to the words that you speak. Through the tone and timbre of your voice and the content of your message, you can create the experience of the singer on the mountain for yourself and others. You can send out a vibration to release trapped and troubled spirits.

Search your heart to determine why you have selected our card today. Do you long for more freedom in your conversations, your relationships, or your work? Do you feel a certain restraint in yourself that distances you from others? Are you imprisoned by your belief system? Are attachments tying you down?

Have courage and release any feelings or situations that lock you away from your Highest Good. If you are in bondage, set yourself free. Through your example others will recognize their own imprisonment and the possibility of freedom.

25

Lepidolite

TRANQUILITY

Lepidolite

TRANQUILITY

Chakra: Crown
Color: Lavender

Tranquility is a heavenly state where worry is a non-concept. In this peaceful environment, you are able to see beyond and avoid the everyday emotional traps that are laid so carefully for you everywhere. You make decisions from a new place of security and Knowing.

Where do you find tranquility in your world? Can you picture a special place where you are overcome with a peaceful feeling? Tranquility requires a quiet space in which to take form. It is not a condition that appears full-grown and complete. It builds on itself.

Through relaxation, meditation, or any quiet time, you can create an entranceway into the Self that will permit tranquility to enter. Through a corridor of lavender light, the essence of tranquility can be drawn into the body for soothing and healing. Tranquility radiates downward and outward from the Crown chakra—the connection between the Ultimate Peace of the Universe and its physical container, your body. Your vessel can absorb as much tranquility as there is psychic space available.

Tranquility provides a favorable environment for healing to occur. Like planting a garden, tranquility prepares the body to receive the seed of health. It also maintains optimal conditions for that seed to grow and heal the entire Self. Tranquility creates a body-state where tumors and ulcers do not grow, where hearts pump without strain, where minds are free of demons.

Tension holds the body in a vice that causes imbalances—too much here, not enough there. Before you know it, your muscles ache, your head or back hurts, your stomach burns. If allowed to continue on this course, organs will suffer and general body deterioration will begin. The final step is physical death.

Is it necessary to act out this gloomy portrayal? Not if you embrace tranquility in your life. Allow us to help. We carry the essence of tranquility on the physical plane.

Hold our stone or card in your hand or place one of them on top on your head. Sit quietly and breath deeply. Enter through the Crown chakra and immerse yourself in the lavender color there. Allow the lavender to flow from the Crown chakra down slowly into your chakra system. Then, release tranquility from each chakra so that it spreads outward into the body from the core to the extremities.

Visualize this peaceful feeling entering your physical self like colored liquid entering water. See the lavender spreading into every pore of your being. You should feel a total relaxation, a letting-go of all your encumbrances. Particularly, you will notice the release of tension in your neck and along your spinal column. Tranquility gently moves out any blockages caused by tension.

You have opened the door to your body and said "Welcome." You have invited the magic of healing into your space. If you do this exercise regularly, you can keep your inner self and body free of any problems.

Why have you drawn our card today? How does tranquility

figure in your life? It is our job to help you understand what an important role tranquility plays in your well-being. If you can create a tranquil life, age will put no physical limitations on you. You will defy common logic with your health and vitality. Emotionally, you will enjoy a serenity that you have never experienced before. Spiritually, you will be able to connect to an unending source of Universal Abundance.

Ordinarily, tranquility and disease do not co-exist. However, there may be some incarnations when the soul has agreed to take on a physical condition for learning. An awareness and understanding of that situation may often be accompanied by a feeling of peace and tranquility.

If you find yourself in a disease state or in an emotional crisis, it is never too late for you to feel the positive effects of tranquility. It is as readily available to you as it is to someone in good health. Even if your physical vehicle is damaged to a point that your physical death is imminent, tranquility will quiet your mind and soothe your soul. Those who love and care for you will be comforted as well. Tranquility, like all vibrational states, is a wave which spreads to all in its immediate proximity and vicariously, through them to the rest of the world.

We long for you to experience inner peace. There is no substitute for what it will bring to your life. Let it become your constant companion, your normal way of being. We are honored to be part of the Crystal Contingent that has wanted for so long to talk to you, our dear and treasured friends.

26

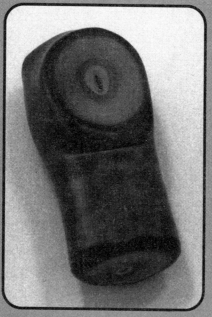

Malachite

EVOLUTION

Malachite

EVOLUTION

Chakra: Heart
Color: Green

The Great Creator intends that you be an active participant in the creation of your destiny. This is the purpose behind Free Will. Free Will is not intended to leave you stranded without guidance to make life's decisions. It is not an abandonment. It is a blessing that makes you a co-creator of Universal Order. Choosing your course in life wisely will impact the Whole in a positive way. None of us is isolated. Every thought, word, or deed affects everything else.

Free Will always allows you the choice of acting or not acting. There are times when you feel you have neither the emotional reserve or physical strength to make major changes. Sometimes doing nothing is the best decision. Non-action is an action of its own.

Other times, even though you would like to put off the inevitable, something within your Soul gnaws at you—a feeling of unrest or agitation. You can feel that that a larger purpose is at work. You know in your heart, that reluctant or not, this is your time. Moving forward is what your soul has chosen now.

Courage is a prerequisite for growth. But if you do not feel particularly brave at this moment, do not worry. Your Higher Self senses within you when you have the strength to accomplish your goals. In addition, you are not alone. Helpers and Guides in the physical and non-physical realms support you.

Often, before you can move forward, it is necessary to do some internal excavation. Are you holding onto any old belief systems that could hold you back?

Like a bulldozer moving earth for new construction, we help you push through any barriers that are blocking your evolution—that inhibit movement and change. We make room for and stimulate new growth. Our deep, green whirlpools spiral within to unearth stagnation and blockage.

If you have chosen our card today, it is because you have made a commitment to uncover the obstacles in your life and make the necessary changes to grow. Even though you consciously want to change, some part of you may be resistant to letting go of old paradigms. We will help you penetrate through layers of resistance so that you can bring any problem areas to the surface. Our green healing energy comes directly from the Heart chakra to comfort and support you as you look at your issues and work through them.

Whether you are facing small changes or life-shaking ones, when they are over, you will not be the same person that you were at the onset. And although it may not appear to be the case, you are always the one initiating the process of change. Yes, even if you were fired from your job, jilted by your lover, or had an accident. Your Higher Self set these emotional earthquakes in motion for your growth.

To truly evolve, there must be a balance of growth and integration. You make changes and then need a time of rest to assimilate and incorporate what you have learned. It is part of the great cyclical nature of the Universe—activity and inactivity, expansion and contraction.

During your time of growth, take time to rest and regenerate while absorbing your new life experiences. Life is balance. Move away from the intensity of this work to lighter, leisure activities. This equilibrium will help you integrate the new person you have worked so hard to become. Congratulations, friend. Our blessings are with you.

27

Moldavite

APPEARANCES

Moldavite

APPEARANCES

Chakra: Heart
Color: Green

Hurtling through space, red-hot to the melting point. Cutting through the atmosphere and plunging deep within the Earth. Finally coming to rest. Feeling the cool of the earth around us as we move into a solid state, so different than we were in our former home. There, we were in constant motion, a moving, active substance. Here we are still and quiet.

We are aliens here, strangers to your planet. It was our mission to make a very long journey to serve as confirmation for you that other worlds exist. The elements in our bodies are entirely different than those of Earth. It was known that scientists familiar with Earth materials would recognize that we came from the stars.

Our external selves are very different from our internal selves. The outer opaque rivulets on our bodies were created by the heat we experienced on our entry. Obscured by our outer selves, our inner selves are a clear, unclouded green. We would be judged as gemstone quality by your Earth standards.

Our core is unflawed and clear, but it is hidden by our outer self. Is it not the same with you? Your smile belies the pain within. A ravaged face may mask the beauty of the soul. A crippled body may disguise untapped abilities.

Our message for you is about appearances. For example, your Star Brothers and Sisters are quite different from you in body shape and substance. Though different on the outside, all entities spring from the same Universal source of love. External appearances have nothing to do with the reality of any situation. What is important is the kernel of truth that lies at the heart.

To see beyond appearances is to look the homeless man in the eye and see the prince. To look beyond appearances is to touch the face of God.

Within, beyond all outer shells, you are pure of heart. And so are all your kin throughout the Universe. Yes, there has been distortion of the basic principles of Love, Truth, and Honor; but underneath it all, when everything else is stripped away, the pure soul appears.

Millions of dollars are spent each year around the world to glorify outer appearances. Regardless of the industry—cosmetics, fashion, plastic surgery, or weight loss—the approach is to fix the external and achieve happiness. But none of it is long lasting.

If the inner self needs nourishment, no amount of feeding the outer will satisfy it. The inner self is the self of beauty. A beauty that has nothing to do with the shape of a face, smooth skin, or a trim body. When will you see it, friends? It pains us so to see you in such misery.

If you have drawn our card today, perhaps you need to reassess the value of appearances. When you look upon us, let it remind you that you are more than your shell. Search for the gemstone within you. You will not have to look far. It is within your generous and kind heart. It is also within the heart of the unusual looking beings you call ETs. It is within those creatures on your planet that you find repugnant. There is beauty there. See the Divine in those you revile. See the luminosity in those whose appearances repel you. They are your family.

We assist your Heart Chakra by helping you accept the alien within yourself. This is the person inside that you deny, whose face or behavior you try to hide. Even the word appearances gives you the clue. To appear implies what something seems to be, not what it is. Do not be fooled by appearances. Look beyond them and within. Reach out to those you would have turned away from before.

There will be one day when you will remember the description of our journey from the stars. You will have a similar experience. Your spirit and soul will be set free and you will leave your physical body behind. That is the point when the outer and inner selves will totally merge. There will be no confusion about which is the real you. You will be pure light and pure love. All beings will look the same. For in truth, we are, even now. Only appearances fool us into thinking that we are different and separate. It is an illusion. We are one.

We have such faith in you, our dear human friends. If your lifetimes were as long as ours on the planet you would know that what is important endures, although appearances may tell you differently.

Love is everywhere. Do not miss it just because it is hiding behind an unattractive exterior. If you look with your heart's eyes you will see it shining through. Sisters and brothers, we love you.

28

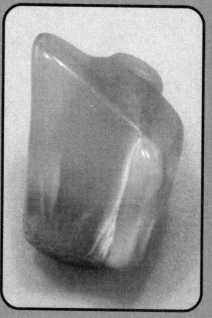

Moonstone

SELF-CONFIDENCE

Moonstone

SELF-CONFIDENCE

Chakra: Crown
Color: White

Each time you take on new challenges and are successful, you have more faith in yourself and your abilities. As a child, staying up on skates for the first time inspired you to think of yourself in an entirely new way. This feeling of competency may have been reinforced by the warm hug and "Well done" of your mother and father.

In the end, others can foster self-confidence, but unless you believe in your own skills and proficiency, the praise that they lavish on you may mean little. Most people do not realize that they have all they need within them to accomplish their goals. Recognizing this Universal Truth can boost your self-confidence one hundred percent.

Perhaps some of your talents have been hidden behind uncertainty or insecurity. You may not have had the encouragement and support that is so important in developing an accurate self-concept. When you see the untapped potential that you had not recognized before, you begin to have confidence in your Self. You realize that you are not the same person you thought you were.

You begin to trust yourself. Your decisions and actions are based on a calm source of strength and self-possession. You maintain an inner counsel with yourself that is not affected by others' opinions of you. Self-confidence results from knowing yourself and respecting what you see. You feel secure in allowing your internal navigation center to take over because you know that it is working from a self-assured, knowledgeable place.

Some people appear to be self-confident on the surface, while inside are terrified of being unseated by the latest competitor in the next business deal, cooking contest, or volleyball game. This fear is based on a distorted view of self-worth that stipulates that you are doing well only if others are doing poorly. In truth, the Universe intends that everyone be a winner. In the material world, there will always be someone who has more than you or who can do something better. They may have a nicer home, more stylish clothes, or a newer and faster car. Perhaps they are smarter, better looking, or a better conversationalist than you.

The talents or successes of others cannot diminish you. Their experiences have nothing to do with you. The material belongings or qualities they possess are their manifestations for their own life story. They relate to you only as opportunities for you to work on any personal issues of inadequacy, insecurity, and self-worth.

Your worth also has nothing to do with bettering an adversary. Your worth resides within your being. It is constructed from the essence of who you truly are—Consummate Goodness. Your true identity emerges anytime you generously and lovingly give of yourself without worrying about the worthiness of your gift. When you are able to see the underlying perfection of your otherwise imperfect outer self, you will be filled with ultimate confidence in your Self.

The white essence of Moonstone echoes the energy of the Crown chakra with which we work. We enable a Universal vibration to occur in which self-confidence can establish itself and take root. To create the proper environment for this infusion of energy, you must relax areas of the body that are holding tension.

As you sit quietly with our stone or our card, let the energy from above move down your chakra system and your spinal column to relax this entire area. Release any tightness in your diaphragm. Feel a quiet serenity filling your entire being. The peacefulness you feel allows us to bathe you in the elixir of self-confidence. Like a warm fluid flowing, self-confidence spreads downward and outward from the Crown chakra.

Self-confidence is experienced in the body as a deep relaxation and absence of worry. It is a feeling of certainty that all is happening as it should and that whatever occurs, you will be able to handle it. You peacefully surrender to the reliability, capability, and dependability of your Essential Self. When you have complete confidence in yourself, what is there to be concerned about?

At this point, you are probably wondering about people and circumstances outside yourself. You can rely on yourself, but what about the rest of existence? Is any of it reliable?

If you can hold within you the quiet assurance that self-confidence offers, the outer world need not concern you. The actions of others and the movings of Fate will be governed by your calm resolve. Everything will move at your rhythm, reaching the successful conclusion that always accompanies self-confidence.

You gain self-confidence about the outer world when you realize that you are in control of it as much as you are of your own self. Your world is filled with safety and well-being, relationships with loving and reliable people, and a harmony and union with the Universe.

Why has our card appeared for you today? Do you want to feel more self-confident in all aspects of your life? Do you need to get to know yourself better before you can feel the surety that self-confidence brings? Do you admire the self-confidence of someone you know and long to be more like them? We encourage you: do not be more like *them*, be more like *you*.

To discover your self-confidence, find out who you are. Determine your strengths and weaknesses, your capacity for love, your own inner knowing, and your ability to set aside others' judgments of you. Explore yourself without fear. Your shortcomings are not shameful or horrible to face. They appear to be imperfections, but are, in reality, new opportunities to grow and experience life. Learn to love yourself just the way you are now. Tomorrow, you can improve; today, accept.

We have confidence in you that you will grow to have confidence in your Self. When you feel the stillness of self-confidence within you, you will have no doubt that everything is possible. You make it possible through the quality of self that you bring to any life situation. Do not be deterred by life's imagined roadblocks, they are not real. Go around them. We send you our love and support as you evolve into your true Self.

29

Obsidian

HONESTY

Obsidian

HONESTY

Chakra: Root
Color: Black

From the bowels of the Earth we greet you, dear friends. We are composed of the fiery lava that rises up from the innermost core of the Earth. You have seen the destruction wrought by a volcano. As in the ancient city of Pompeii, all that lies within the path of the lava flow is cleansed by fire.

There is a cleansing that occurs deep within the core of the human self of no lesser consequence. The Root chakra is the point in the physical self where Kundalini energy rises through the chakra system clearing the way for illumination and enlightenment. This purging of the self is accomplished as all pretense is stripped away and is replaced by total honesty.

Like the lava from which we are made, we cut through anything that blocks the path of truth. There is no hiding from self when we work together. We create an environment for you to look honestly at who you are, and how you conduct your life. We wish you no discomfort. No cruelty or pain is intended. It is simply our mission to serve as a mirror of truth.

If you have drawn our card today, ask yourself some hard questions. Are you really honest with yourself? How about with others? When friends ask your opinion or advice, do you tell them what you think they want to hear instead of the truth? You may be trying to be kind. Perhaps you do not want to hurt their feelings. Or you may be afraid that if you are honest they will no longer like you.

Every time you tell a lie, you tell yourself a second lie that it is OK to be dishonest. You say, "It was only a little white lie." In this way, you hope to justify that it was not malicious or harmful. You have probably never given any thought to what effect one lie may have on the entire Universe.

Lies create an actual veil that clouds reality from humans. This is a difficult concept to comprehend. It is difficult to explain. The act of dishonesty creates a fog-like trance state which obscures the true purpose of humans on the planet.

During the course of the evolution of this planet, there have been those who have set into motion certain scenarios to control humans. Illusions were created that kept all of humanity from seeing the beauty and truth of life. One of the most successful devices has been the use of emotional states to confuse, to distract, and to detour.

Lies are an emotional tool that contributes to the deception. Dishonesty is not the only culprit. Greed, hate, intolerance, and other emotional conditions are designed to separate you from one another and keep you from your mission here. Now is the time to break this patterning so that humans can reclaim their power and see the reality of their existence and their purpose.

You can make a contribution of enormous magnitude by deciding today to be honest with yourself and those around you. Start in small ways. There are opportunities everyday to choose to tell the truth instead of a lie.

Someone asks, "How are you?" Usually, you say, "Fine." The next time it happens, if you are not doing so well, say, "Well, I've had better days." It is true, most people are just being sociable and may not want to hear how you are in the first place. The point is that you will have an opportunity to speak honestly. By doing so, you also get more in touch with how you are really feeling.

When you decide to hold onto a lie, you have to devote an enormous amount of energy to remembering the exact details surrounding it. You also spend some additional energy worrying over having to deal with a confrontation about the lie or simply having to retell it one more time. Whether a small lie or a big one, you are holding actual pockets of energy within your psyche that take up emotional and spiritual space and weigh you down.

How do you want to spend your time? Being creative, having fun, helping someone, or nursing some lie? What a waste of the magnificent being you are. Stop carrying around the energy required by a lie. Feel the release of that energy that the truth brings. You are fond of saying, "The truth shall set you free." The fact that you use this phrase indicates that your collective unconscious remembers correctly an essential wisdom. Honesty is liberating.

Some humans find the game of deception exciting and seductive. They may juggle any number of intricately woven dramas at the same time to see how much they can get away with. They may even *fool all of the people all of the time*. But ultimately the greatest damage they do is to themselves.

The truth is how things really are. A lie is an entanglement that strangles the human spirit and kills integrity. Observe the times that in thought, word, and deed, you are truthful to yourself and to others. Your gift will be a heart free of guilt and full of light.

239

An honest life is an honorable life. The courage you exhibit in being honest will inspire others to be the same. The power of your honesty will reverberate across the Universe. In the spirit of truth, we are your friends.

30

Ojo Caliente
Timekeepers

HARMONY

Ojo Caliente Timekeepers

HARMONY

Chakra: Crown
Color: White/Gray

I am the Deva of Ojo Caliente, New Mexico. I have been invited to speak by the Deva of the Timekeepers and I will take my turn before my stone kin. I want you to understand about our home. I want to paint a beautiful picture of it in your minds.

Our Canyon was formed thousands of years ago. The waters rushed forward and carved the deep ravine where the river now runs and the winds sweep through. Civilizations have come and gone. Many humans have spent their lives here.

Ojo Caliente is a sacred place. In all parts of the world, there are areas where energy pours into a spiral center. This is one of them. These sites form the heart of a region, or in some cases, a country.

In these Earth Temples where vortices spiral, a vertical passageway connects outer space and inner space. Energy flows outward from the Earth and inward from the Universe and merges completely along the way.

Think of it as a dialysis of energy between the Cosmos and the Earth. The result is a cleansing—of body, mind, and, especially, spirit. To you, the experience would feel like a cool breeze blowing against your face and through your soul.

243

In Ojo Caliente, on the physical plane, underground tributaries and springs from around the area converge. Just as your human heart pumps blood throughout your body, the waters of Ojo Caliente energize and enliven this area. Humans come for the healing and purifying properties of the water, and, on more subtle levels, the energy.

All beings are welcome to come here for healing. But the business of "the Healing Waters" will never be allowed to become too profitable. This area will never become a theme park. Ojo Caliente is a center for harmony. No human venture will compromise the purpose of Ojo Caliente. I am the Watcher. I am its Guardian. I will preserve its sanctity.

Devas and Nature Spirits of all kinds gather here. We join for a communion of Spirit and experience. We come together to safeguard the harmony of all life everywhere. We combine our collective energy to restore equilibrium to the Earth's core.

The Ancient Ones, whose hearts beat in unison with the earth, recognized the sacredness gathered here. They made their settlements on the cliffs above the river, not only for its physical advantages, but the spiritual ones as well.

I have always enjoyed the tinkling sound of humans working and playing cooperatively. When humans disagree and become violent, their music sounds like a discordant orchestra. Everyone playing the wrong note at the wrong time. Except for this vibration, our canyon, river, and cliffs have enjoyed harmony and tranquility through the ages. Now that you know about this beautiful haven, my stone friends will tell you more.

We, the Ojo Caliente Timekeepers, lived upon the cliffs where many human communities have dwelt. There, they grew their crops, made their pottery, saw the dawn and dusk of their physical sojourn. For the most part, they were peaceful peoples.

Humans did not always arrive with peaceful intentions, but once here they found that they could not help themselves. The calming energy of this area soothed their anger and quieted their tempers. Ojo Caliente helped them settle their differences and arrive at peaceful accord.

Whenever negative human emotions reared their noisy heads here, the wind of harmony played over them. The natural and only choice was to come to agreement. Any other option would have introduced a cacophony that would have shattered their existence. Literally, the discord would have vibrated the patterns of this physical existence so that it would have broken like a pane of glass. These peoples could not have imagined the specific effect of their disharmony, but they intuitively sensed the potential, final outcome—their doom and an end to their bliss.

Cooperation is reached through harmony. First, there must be inner, individual harmony. A sense of balance. A feeling of peace. Once inner harmony is achieved, no one would risk losing it. As a natural instinct, you would strive to perpetuate that harmony with your family and neighbors.

If the effects of discordance are so destructive to the environment, imagine the effect on the human self. Today, in your world, you are constantly bombarded by the vibrations of hate, fear, anger, jealousy, and greed. As a result, and perhaps with good reason, you distrust your fellow humans, making cooperation impossible.

Your body is an instrument being played by this destructive music.

After a while these vibrations accumulate and need venting. These negative emotions get acted out in arguments at one extreme, escalating to riots, mayhem, and murder at the other.

No matter how powerful these forces, they are not nearly so powerful as the heart centers of the Earth joined by your individual hearts in harmony. With cooperation as a foundation, Intergalactic and Earth beings have formed a web of protection around the planet, a safety net of love and peace. We reflect the energy of the Crown chakra through our color and vibration to help connect you with this Universal essence.

Will all negativity completely disappear? Unfortunately, no. But it does not have to touch you. You can neutralize its effect and rob it of its intent and power through harmony in your interactions.

Why have you drawn our card today? How is the issue of harmony impacting your life? Do you want to create harmony internally by resolving conflicting emotions? Do you want to foster harmonious, cooperative relationships with your family, friends, or co-workers?

Treat your fellow beings and yourself with kindness and reverence. Discord cannot exist where there is mutual respect and tolerance. If you are met with animosity, counter it with love. *Turn the other cheek.* Set the example. The Whole will prosper as a result.

A special kind of music needs to be played throughout the Universe. It is the melody of Love. You are an instrument of the Light. Together, we all form the Orchestra of Life. The harmonic symphony of our collaboration can heal us individually and collectively.

We have spoken to enlist your help for all entities, and for our Home, Planet Earth. Join us and the other Kingdoms in a reunion of cooperation to preserve all that we have accomplished together. We bless you and thank you for your help.

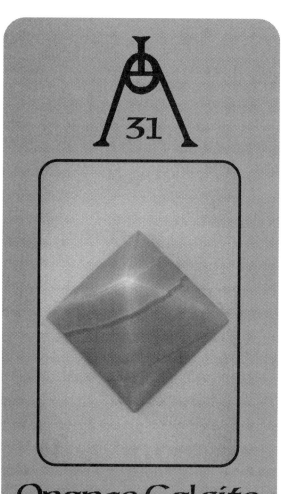

31

Orange Calcite

FULFILLMENT

Orange Calcite

FULFILLMENT

Chakra: Sacral
Color: Orange

Fulfillment is a state of bliss that occurs when you are being completely who you are and doing exactly what you are meant to do. When you make a commitment to yourself to seek and speak the Highest Truth and to give and receive the Highest Good, fulfillment results.

However, fulfillment may seem like an illusion, if, instead of commitment, your life is full of obligations. People often confuse these two concepts. Although often used almost interchangeably, they are not the same. Obligation implies that you feel compelled to do something that you might rather not. Commitment is a dedication of the soul's time, resources, and energy to an intention. It is a joyful, not a belabored, giving of oneself.

If you spend your days obligated by work and family responsi-bilities, home and car maintenance, and activity scheduling, you may become resentful and unhappy. You are probably thinking that most of these tasks are unavoidable. Of course, there are many responsibilities you need to honor. But do you ever take on obligations unnecessarily to fill your time and avoid looking at and really living your life. Even with all there is to occupy your time, is something missing? Have you ever thought, "Is this all there is?"

Think about the words *spend your time*. To spend implies that you have certain resources that may at some point be used up. Time is one of these resources. You have only so many days on this planet as the person you are now. We encourage you to spend your time wisely. Do not waste a moment.

For your happiness—and for the example that you set for your children, family, and friends—we urge you to examine the quality of your life. Many of you are convinced that if each day is packed with activities, your life is full. In fact, your life is not full, it is just filled up. With all this filling, are you *fulfilled?* More is not necessarily fulfilling, it may just be more.

What can you do to bring joy and meaning into your life? In some cases, your activities may have to stay the same, but you may approach them differently through introspection and a new attitude. In other circumstances, upon examination, you may find that it is necessary for responsibilities to shift so that you can have a life among all your activities.

The first commitment you make must be to yourself. If you are living a life of purpose and fulfillment, all around you will benefit. If you are not, you will be unhappy and that, too, will affect everyone that you touch.

Why have you drawn our card today? What guidance are you seeking? Are you looking for the treasure trove of fulfillment? What will it look like when you find it? Do you wonder how you can contribute to the fulfillment of others? What will make your heart sing?

Your mission this lifetime is valuable to the well-being of all and the survival of Planet Earth. You need not be a great scientist, artist, or orator. You may find your special work driving daily carpools, inspiring young children to treat each other with respect and love. Your mission may be to stand up against discrimination that you encounter in your workplace. Your purpose may be to fill soup bowls at a homeless shelter.

Each of us in the Universe has a calling. This *calling* is a beckoning of our souls to explore how we can inspire or help others. There are countless ways that love and caring can express themselves. One of our purposes is to be here speaking with you to let you know how priceless are the gifts you have to offer.

We are the orange companion of the Second or Sacral chakra, designed to help you tap into this center of creativity to fashion your life of fulfillment. To find your calling, you must look and listen with the eyes and ears of your soul. Where you see need, offer help. If you long for fulfillment, you will find it in the grateful smiles of others you have comforted. You will see it in the eyes of a stray animal you have fed. You will experience it when you realize that you are making a positive difference in the world.

Fulfillment is waiting for you to discover it. Fulfill yourself in such a way that more love and compassion will be spread throughout the Earth and the Universe. Each of us has unique gifts to offer. Use your special gifts to fill your heart and illuminate the lives of others. Bless you, friend.

32

Rhodochrosite

SELF-WORTH

Rhodochrosite

SELF-WORTH

Chakra: Heart
Color: Pink

You have been given life because you have special gifts to contribute to the world. Your real worth is not dependent upon how much you earn, what you wear, or how you look. Your value lies in your unique individuality.

It does not matter whether others see your talents. You may not even recognize them yourself. Your talents were given to you by the Creator. Your gifts are so special that you have been created as an individual entity to accommodate them. They differentiate you from all other beings.

You may think that you serve no purpose here. This is not true. Without you, the Universe is incomplete and could not function in proper order. You may not know your purpose, but you have one. Continue to look inside your heart, and you will discover why you are here.

Your worth also has nothing to do with others' opinions of you. Realizing this is the first step to self-love. When you let go of the judgments others have forced upon you, you will begin to recognize your worthiness. As long as you agree with and perpetuate any judgments that find you lacking, you can not love yourself. Self-love can not exist with self-deprecation.

Many of you have been told cruel things about yourself—that you were stupid, ugly, or worthless. These words were spoken by those who have lost touch with their souls. They were perpetuating the hurt that they had felt in their own life. Consequently, they could not allow themselves to see your beautiful and special light.

When humans are in pain, they strike out. The critical thing to remember is that their anger probably has nothing to do with you. Others' reactions toward you have to do with *them,* not *you.* Unfortunately, you just happened to be nearby when a wounded person attacked.

As you begin to love yourself, free of judgment, healing will occur. You will mend the injuries you have suffered from the thoughtlessness of others. As you welcome yourself home, you will feel the connectedness to all other beings and love them free of judgment as well. A new strength will empower you to move forward with kindness to others and to yourself.

You cannot truly love others until you love yourself. This is the responsibility and challenge we place before you—to recognize the perfect being that dwells within.

Why have you drawn the Rhodochrosite card today? Our pink essence blends with the Heart chakra to help you realize how lovable and worthwhile you are. Perhaps this is a time when you are unable to see your beautiful soul and recognize your value. Maybe you have gotten yourself into a romantic relationship or job situation where you are being taken for granted or treated abusively.

Once you truly appreciate the beautiful creature that you are, you will be reluctant to enter into or remain in any circumstances that are unhealthy or destructive. Learn to say no. Do not let others hurt you. Do not hurt yourself. You deserve the most respectful treatment.

Take care of *yourself.* You take care of others—your children, your parents, your spouse. But what about you? You often put yourself last. What message does this send about how you value yourself?

We encourage you to put yourself first. That may sound selfish to you. Are we suggesting that you neglect someone else to take care of yourself? Of course not. However, if you do not honor yourself and your needs, how will you have the emotional or physical energy to help others?

Some of your financial institutions encourage you to "pay yourself first." They want you to reserve some of your cash in a savings account. When you take time for yourself, you are depositing energy into an emotional or physical account that you will need to draw on later. When demands are placed on you, if you have put nothing away, your coffers will be empty.

In addition, you are a model for those around you. Your family and friends will learn a valuable lesson about self respect from watching you take the necessary time to maintain your well-being. If others observe you treating yourself with respect, they will probably treat you and themselves the same way.

Real survival is more than mere physical existence. It is a healthy, positive quality of life without dysfunction. Imagine the possibilities for a species that refuses to be victims or victimizers.

There are no criteria for your self-worth. You are worthy, regardless. Treat yourself with the love and acceptance you deserve. Fill your heart with forgiveness towards yourself and those who have hurt you. Let go of blame, resentment, and bitterness.

We offer ourselves to assist in the healing of your wounded self. You were meant to be whole, loving, and joyful. And you will be. And you are. Bless you.

33

River Rock

ALLOWING

Riɑer Rock

ALLOWING

Chakra: Root
Color: Dark Gray

Through the years, gentle waves lapping round us and wild torrents pounding upon us have carved us into smooth, rounded stones. We have no sharp edges. We offer ourselves as an example to humans of the shedding of layers, the rough edges that develop through your many emotional hard knocks.

You were created smooth. Over time, disappointment, rejection, and fear formed callouses as a type of protection to soften life's blows. That hardened shield has served you well. It has warned others against hurting you and they have backed away. The armor protects you, but it also isolates you.

It takes courage to risk letting go of the roughness and toughness that protects you from others. Why should you give them an opening by exposing that soft underbelly where you are vulnerable? Because loneliness is a high price to pay for safety. The dropping of your guard will bring you closer to others and remove you from self-imposed isolation.

Rough edges and jagged points threaten. One of the reasons we allow the water to wear away our tough exteriors is to be more accessible to the Human Kingdom. Humans who wade the river's edges consider our smooth surface friendly. They are not afraid of us. We offer ourselves as a place for them to step, to sit, to rest tired bodies and spirits.

If you have drawn this card today, the message for you may be to let the emotional waters of life wash over you. Allow yourself to resurrect an old hurt with the intent of letting it go. Permit yourself the vulnerability of really feeling the emotion. Then, release it to the river of life to be swept away. Free yourself of it. The situation itself was painful enough. Your pain has been multiplied by forcing it down for so long.

You are brave to risk the temporary pain that a face-to-face confrontation with an old demon may cause. The act of allowing the pain to surface, working through it, and then releasing it will free you and soothe your soul. Next time it will not be so hard. You will notice that as you are willing to be more vulnerable, you will pose less of a threat to others. They will approach you more often and serve as a support system for you.

Another message that we bring is to "go with the flow." Sometimes life presents challenges that you have no control over—a divorce, a job loss, an illness. Your immediate reaction may be to get angry. "Why me?" you ask.

When it appears as though there is truly nothing you can do to affect your situation, the wisest course may be to surrender to it. In your world, the word *surrender* has many negative connotations. It is what you do after you have lost a war. In your experience, surrender means submission, capitulation, and impotency. In reality, the opposite is true.

Surrender in its truest sense does not mean giving up. It means allowing what is occurring to be part of your life process instead of denying it. Learn from the experience. Figure out its message.

Our dark gray energy blends with that of the Root chakra, the place of merging of the physical body with the planet. We and the First chakra offer a healing and grounding connection with our foundation and protector, Mother Earth.

We are designed to be in the flow of the river. You are designed to be in the flow of life. The more either of us resists, the more we block the soothing waters from gentling us. Be brave, friend.

Rose Quartz

FORGIVENESS

Rose Quartz

FORGIVENESS

Chakra: Heart
Color: Pink

Forgive yourself, dear friend. Those of you in the Human Kingdom find so much for which to blame yourselves. At the heart of the blaming is an unrealistic goal for perfection and the fear of falling short of that goal.

Deep in your soul is the memory of the perfect state of love and unity you felt long ago on your journey through time and space. You have not forgiven yourself for forgetting how to return to that place of infinite love.

Your journey here in the physical is not a fall from Grace as your religions would have you believe. Rather, it is another medium or environment for you to work on different soul aspects. Physical incarnation on Earth is an opportunity that only a limited number of souls may experience. The waiting line is long to travel the road you currently walk.

And yet, there are many times when you would prefer to give up this existence—to be relieved of the responsibility and the suffering of your experience here. Believe us, Dear One, this Earthly sojourn is a gift.

Cherish each moment of every day with thankfulness for this opportunity. For, on Earth, you experience the connectedness of spirituality and emotion translated into the physical. The caring touch, the friendly smile, the supportive hug, the passionate embrace, are treasures available to you. This is love made tangible—for your pleasure, for the warming and gentling of your heart, for your soul growth.

You often say, "I'm only human." Forgive yourself for being human. To be human is not a curse. It is a blessing. To be *only* human is a Universal miracle.

Because of negative conditioning, many humans have forgotten their inherent perfection. It seems that no matter how hard you try, whatever you achieve never appears to be good enough. Consequently, you spend your entire life trying to make up for your perceived failings. Here is the Truth: you are not a failure. You have chosen this physical life to learn. You are here figuring out what works and what does not. If you knew all you needed to, you would not be here.

This incarnation is not the time to worry about perfection. This is the time for moving forward and releasing old patterns that no longer work. Now is the time for taking stock of where you stand in your life and changing course if you feel empty, unhappy, or disconnected. This is the time for recognizing yourself as a beautiful, loving, and lovable being with much to offer.

If you have drawn this card today, consider those that you need to forgive. Make a list of the people who you feel have wronged you in some way. It might include your parents or family members who did not treat you kindly. Perhaps you resent them for not preparing you properly for the difficult demands that the world would place on you.

You may also think of friends who were disloyal or turned

against you when you needed them most. At the top of the list may be a lover or a spouse who had committed to a relationship of caring and trust and who has disappointed or abandoned you. Or, are you angry at yourself for some perceived deficiency?

Mentally hold these people in your mind, including yourself, and open your heart to each one. Speak to them. Tell them that you forgive them and release them from your resentment. Let them know that you see that they are trying, like you are, to find out how to live in a very challenging and confusing world. Tell them that you know that they are wounded too.

Surround them in White Light and bless them on their journey here. After you have sent them all the love that is in your heart, take the list and burn it with the flame from a white candle. This act symbolizes your letting them go. You no longer hold them, or yourself, in emotional bondage. Automatically, the weight lifts from your shoulders. Your heart is open, free, and filled with love.

Our work with you is about lifting the heavy, oppressive mantle of bitterness and blame. The freedom that results from forgiveness loosens the cords constricting the Heart chakra. Each time you forgive, the restrictive emotional cords around the Planet are also loosened. More love can then flow to heal each individual soul and the Earth's soul as well. We send our pink ray into your heart with love and blessings, human sisters and brothers.

35

Rutilated Quartz

NURTURANCE

Rutilated Quartz

NURTURANCE

Chakra: Solar Plexus/Crown
Color: Gold/Clear

You are never alone. The Universe and Mother Earth are your guardians, always at your side. A guardian's responsibility is to watch over and foster those in its care. A guardian is a protector, an agent, always looking out for its ward's best interests—providing the environments and experiences which you need for learning and growth.

Guardian Angels and other beings, called Guides, are special emissaries from the Universe that share the responsibility of helping you through each incarnation. They prepare the way and clear a path for you.

The wealth that your Guides provide comes in many guises. It might be financial in nature—an inheritance, a contest jackpot, or a raise. It also takes other forms of fulfillment—romantic love, health, a happy family, a rewarding profession, friends, or peace of mind. With this Universal wealth, there is no lack or emptiness. As you prosper, you live well, you do well, and you are well. You are in the fullness of well-being.

In the human vehicle, the awareness of emptiness and fullness resides in the Solar Plexus or Third chakra The Third chakra is located just above your navel near the stomach. If you are feeling hunger, your "gut" will tell you so. But what kind of hunger is it?

The physical vehicle asks, "Is there food and water?" The emotional self asks, "Is there love?" The soul asks, "Is there peace?"

Are you currently dealing with an emotional or spiritual emptiness in your life? You may notice that along with other feelings of distress, you feel physically empty as well. This hollow feeling causes many people to eat when they are unhappy and is at the heart of eating disorders. Those who eat to fill this void feel as though they are literally going to starve to death. On a conscious level, they may not understand the reason they are driven to eat. It is not self-indulgence or weakness of character, it is an act of survival.

In the womb, most of you had no concern about your well-being. Your mother provided your nourishment for you. Her body was your safe harbor. The last time you may have felt real security might have been in the womb. Once out in the world, physically separated from your provider, you doubted whether your meals would appear when you needed them. Perhaps someone else's bodily demands would dictate when you would be fed.

This anxiety carried over into childhood. And later, into adulthood, where it mutated into generalized feelings of uncertainty about whether your needs would be met. Now, when you are hungry, you experience unconscious anxiety similar to the kind you had as a baby. Even though a full stomach is as close as the next fast food restaurant, your concern lies much deeper.

The nourishment you need most does not come from physical food. What you crave is "Manna from Heaven," the caregiving that outpours from the Universe to you—Cosmic TLC. Once you are filled with the nurturance that the Universe provides, there will be no gnawing in your belly. Knowing you are cared for and cared about will quiet the hunger pains.

We are a collective, a mineral combining clear quartz and the golden fibers of rutile. We hold the colors and energies of both the Crown and the Solar Plexus chakras. The Crown chakra is a special connecting point where Universal nourishment pours into the body. The Solar Plexus chakra is the location that absorbs the Sun's energy, like a solar collector.

Working together, we are a superconductor of energy, a conduit between these two power plants allowing humans to draw Cosmic Soul Food into the body. We are a physical embodiment of Universal nutriment.

Why have you drawn our card today? Do you have concerns about your well-being? Do you wonder if you will be OK? Many of you feel adrift, without any real support. Most of you are wishing that someone would say, "Everything will be alright." The Universe can be that loving friend.

Perhaps you feel well-nurtured and could serve as a benefactor for someone else. Is there some individual or group that you could support? There are many beings in our world who are defenseless and who need your help. Try to imagine the empty, panicky feeling of need or desperation that they may be experiencing.

If there is some creature you can bring under your protection, please do so. Although the Universe provides for all its children, it gives us ample opportunity to help others and thereby experience the role of nurturer and friend.

It is the way of the Universe that each of us is to be the nurturer and the nurtured, the protector and the one protected, the giver and the receiver. This is the Law of Universal Reciprocity, the great harmonizer and equalizer. Move into the Divine Flow to assist and be assisted as needs dictate. We stand ready to be your special friend.

36

Selenite

TOLERANCE

Selenite

TOLERANCE

Chakra: Crown
Color: Clear

The Millennium is a turn of the century phenomenon that is always the cause of celebration and much Universal merriment. It heralds the passing from one age to the next. More than simply a date on the calendar, it is a redirection of energy in the Universe and on the planet that will affect every living entity. Nothing will remain the same.

The Millennium that began the Piscean Age was ushered in by the Master Jesus. The Christ, as you called him, spoke of love for all, regardless of outer differences. His messages have endured for two thousand years. And although millions have worshipped him, his words did not have the impact that was intended.

Yes, people attend holy places of worship. Yes, people profess to be righteous. Still, most humans do not love unconditionally. Humans love selectively. If someone is of an *acceptable* color, gender, religion, ethnic background, or philosophy, then they may be found worthy of love. Even in your own families, love is earned. Good behavior, good grades, expectations met, may earn love. Few are loved because of who they are. Instead, they are loved because of what they *do*. Was this Jesus' message?

The New Age that is upon us now is an opportunity to manifest these ancient teachings. As a relatively new mineral on the planet, we have come at this special time of transformation to move into

273

a spiritual maturity with you. Our message is one of tolerance. A tolerance of self and a tolerance of others. This is the Age in which the, so called, Holy wars will come to an end. The practice of killing people who do not look like you or do not agree with you will cease.

Humans will begin to see their fellow men and women as reflections of the Whole. The external will no longer matter. You will look into the hearts and minds of your fellow humans and feel their intentions. A person will always be presumed worthy of love.

If someone falls from high ideals, they will be treated with kindness and understanding. They will not be punished by rejection. They will gently and thoughtfully be shown where they went astray. Your rules of law state that someone will be presumed innocent until proven guilty. Do most people practice this doctrine of non-judgment?

Why have you selected our card today? As you read this passage, are there people or situations that pop into your mind? These images are trying to help you connect with an issue of tolerance.

Have you been intolerant of someone or yourself? Or did you experience the intolerance of another? If so, how did it feel? Try to imagine the feeling of the persistent intolerance that those of different colors, religions, physical appearances, sexual preferences, or nationalities experience when in unfamiliar territory. The next time you feel intolerant, remember what it feels like to be ridiculed, scorned, or ignored just because you are different.

An important key to tolerance involves letting go of judgment. Try relating to family, friends, and yourself with fewer judgments about what is appropriate, valuable, or worthy. Extend this attitude to strangers.

Tolerance is true charity—giving from the heart. You have a saying that "Charity begins at home." You cannot get more at home than under your own skin. If you can develop true tolerance of yourself, tolerance of others will be easy.

We assist the Crown chakra in helping you realize that rigidly-held requirements for acceptability serve no purpose other than to build a wall between you and others. Our clear, crystalline body is a reminder to seek clarity surrounding your acceptance of others and yourself.

Extend your perimeter of tolerance to include everyone, whether they appear to meet your standards or not. Reexamine the arbitrary guidelines you have established to measure someone or something's value. Have you set up an internal credit check to determine the worthiness of others or yourself?

If you were forced to decide which of your beliefs were important enough to die for, your list would probably decrease measurably. Make a commitment to drop at least five nonsensical requirements that you place on yourself or others. If you are using certain criteria to determine what or who is suitable, you are probably isolating yourself from loved ones and strangers.

Our love and tolerance go out to you. We have faith that you will open your hearts to others without conditions. Let your tolerance begin today. Do not wait for the year 2000. You have God's grace within you. We watch over you, our dear friends of the Human Kingdom.

37

Septarian
Nodules

PURPOSE

Septarian Nodules

PURPOSE

Chakra: Root
Color: Brown and White

You probably have never seen or heard of us before. We are being found in the Great Lakes on the planet—in America, in South America, Europe, and Asia. In the distant past, we had a different composition than we do now. In more recent years, we have undergone a process of transformation that has linked the Mineral Kingdom and the Element of Water. We are participating in a joint project with our friends, the Overlighting Deva of Water and the Water Spirits of key lakes on the planet.

These lakes are energy nodes. Our name, nodules, comes from nodes. Septarian relates to the power of the number seven and a seven-cycle process. This process is time and spatially oriented to trigger a network of energy and light across the planet. A preparation is in progress so that more light can be carried within the planet and by all beings on the planet. This gathering of light is one of the many celebrations marking the approach of the Millennium.

Physically, we are brown, the color of your Root chakra and of the soil, the heart of the earth. As minerals age, they disintegrate into soil which can be used for planting. This evolution of our Kingdom is designed to provide food and healing substances for the Animal and Human Kingdoms. It is also part of another cooperative program to assist the Plant Kingdom in fulfilling its mission. The Animal, Plant, and Mineral Kingdoms are always helping each other. We find that whatever we accomplish, there is a qualitative difference for the better when we work together, instead of, separately.

Although the process is imperceptible to the human eye, Water Spirits, in lakes and waterfalls, effect a physical change in us by whirling—spiralling faster than the speed of light. The Devas of the Lakes hold the space for this to occur.

Lasered into our brown surface are inscriptions from the Water Spirits. Each has a message for the humans we find. The messages are linked to the same network of communication as that of the Crop Circles. Although our information is not geometric, it is a different encryption of the same language.

The white markings on our bodies are pure light frozen in stone. Some of these engravings resemble cave pictographs that were created by star travelers and early humans. Many of us have been imprinted with a likeness of the water spirit who carved us. Our stone pictographs are a mode of communication through which we are trying to reach you.

We were seeded here millions of years ago by star travelers. They left us as transmitting devices with whom they could establish contact after they had departed. We have not been used as transmitters for a very long time. Over the millennia, our original purpose must have been forgotten by those who placed us here. We did not realize it at first, but we had forgotten our purpose here too. We had forgotten that we even had a purpose. We existed and by definition that existence indicated that we had value. That was all we knew.

It took us a while to realize that we did have a mission to fulfill. Once we remembered that, we felt better knowing that there was a specific reason we had come to Earth. On the other hand, we felt bad that we could not remember what it was. We did not have a sense of ourselves. It seemed that we were drifting. We felt isolated because we were different.

Over time we came to see that coming into yourself does not happen on one particular, quiet, rainy afternoon. It is a process that occurs over time. Gradually, you discover yourself engaged in totally different thinking and feeling modes that you have never experienced before. Then it occurs to you that you have changed.

The Overlighting Deva of the Mineral Kingdom wanted us to share our story with you because our histories are similar. You were endowed by our Creator with a grand purpose. Each of you has a purpose individually, and, as part of a group, collectively, like us.

The Deva thought that if you heard our story, you would be reminded of your own life. You may not know where you are going or what your purpose is, but you have a valuable role to play, day-by-day, while you are waiting for it to be revealed.

It is the quality of how you spend your days that makes up your life. We decided that even though we did not remember why we were here, we wanted to contribute whatever we could, whatever was needed. Almost as soon as we did that, our reason for being emerged. It was through living a life that benefitted everyone that we felt peace and our concern disappeared. Who we were and why we were here unfolded as a result of joining with the rest of existence to create the highest possible good for all.

It seems as though, to solve a problem, you would need to concentrate continuously on it. Actually, it was through losing our focus on ourselves that we received the information that we needed. We encourage you not to spend your life grieving over what you do not have, all the while missing out on all you do.

Life is waiting for you to get involved. Reach out to your neighbor in friendship. Lend a helping hand to someone or some cause. The more you live Life, the more Life there is to live.

If you have drawn this card today, it may be a sign that it is time to stop worrying about your purpose here. Perhaps you have been too narrowly focused on finding the right answers. No effort is necessary. You do not need to go looking for answers. The answers that you seek will find you.

Committing yourself to the good of all beings everywhere is the key. Sincere interest and involvement come from the heart. And the heart opens all doors. The path to your special work will unfold before you. Not through difficult labor, but through trusting that all will work in your life for your good and your growth.

It is time for individuation and group consciousness to merge— for there to be concern for the whole, rather than just for the self. Part of our work is to help you become aware of this concept. Selflessness does not mean that you will lose your individuality. It will make you more of who you really are. It will magnify the kindness, gentleness, and love inside you.

Most of us in our Kingdom do not have an individual mission or individual karma. As a group soul we have a natural instinct to work for the Greater Good. Being highly individuated, most of you are concerned with the welfare of key people around you, but are not always as conscious of the well-being of all lifeforms.

We realize that to be outwardly-focused rather than inwardly-focused requires a shift in consciousness for humans. You are not selfish because you are self-centered. Individuation has been imprinted on you as strongly as group consciousness has been on us.

It is not yet time for us to share our specific work with you, but we feel privileged to share our story. That is part of our mission too. We have volunteered for this project of service. It is an honor for us to commemorate the coming of a New Age by assisting our human friends.

Let our words serve as encouragement to you. Through losing yourself, you will find yourself. We will be here to offer assistance whenever you need us. Reach out and feel our companionship. We bless you in living each day to the fullest and giving yourself to the World.

38

Smoky Quartz

PROTECTION

Smoky Quartz

PROTECTION

Chakra: Root
Color: Brown

Our role is one of safe-keeping and we are honored to act as your guardian. The physical world can be a harsh environment. Often you are subjected to negative and angry vibrations which can drag you down, depress you, and physically make you ill. We operate like a filter which removes these toxic substances and creates a buffer of energy between you and the outside. Even those dark energies you conjure up yourself can be transmuted through us.

When you are feeling emotionally threatened, carry a piece of Smoky Quartz with you and notice how you glide through uncomfortable situations easily and unharmed. The varying hues of brown that make up our color range are the color of earth and have the same grounding qualities. It is our nature to absorb discordant energies and, like a lightning rod, ground them into the Earth where they are neutralized. During this entire process, you are protected from any negativity.

We intercede when primitive fears surface—those having to do with security and survival. We assist the Root chakra as it acts as a connecting point between you and the energy of the Earth. The Earth's energy field can quickly restore equilibrium when panic and distress intrude upon your life.

We also serve as an example of what you can accomplish for

yourself. You have the ability to surround yourself with an energy field that can absorb the shocks of human existence. We are only helpers, you are the one with the real power. You are completely capable of protecting yourself.

When you find yourself in an emotional situation, visualize an energy shield encircling your physical body, glowing and pulsing. Notice that although you are fully interacting with another person, you are untouched by any negativity that is sent your way. Rather than reacting out of fear to negative vibrations that you feel, you can respond with love and neutralize the negativity.

You will also be able to find a calm, centered place within yourself which will allow you to determine what is really going on. There is a good chance that real, honest communication can occur under these circumstances. And is that not a primary goal for human interaction?

You can also soothe yourself by connecting physically with the Earth. Go outside, sit upon the ground or a rock, let the healing rhythms of the Planet slow your pace and tune you to its own vibration, one of stability and balance.

What are some of the possible reasons you have chosen our card today? You may find yourself in a situation at work or at home that has become emotionally challenging. You may be feeling more vulnerable than usual. You may need reassurance that you are safe and that your world is intact. You may anticipate that an emotional "lion's den" is in your immediate future and feel the need for added security. You may be looking for a peaceful sanctuary in a time of chaos.

Or are you having difficulty with the concept of negativity in general? Light and Darkness are mere manifestations of the duality and polarity of the Universe. They are the Yin and the Yang. Both are necessary; both have a job to do. The mission of Darkness is equally as valuable as that of the Light. To think otherwise is a misconception that has been created and perpetuated by the Human Kingdom. Goodness and Godness is in all—the Darkness and the Light.

When you meet a negative manifestation or darkness in yourself or others, be understanding and appreciative. It provides a lesson that the Light cannot teach you.

You have many friends looking out for your welfare. You are a valued being. You are treasured. The Universe watches over you while it guides you to experiences that will provide you optimal growth and fulfillment.

The energy of protection conveyed to you by our card is ready to support you in any circumstance in which you find yourself. We welcome the opportunity to be your friend and advocate. May the blessings of reassurance and serenity be with you.

Sugilite

OPENNESS

Sugilite

OPENNESS

Chakra: Third Eye
Color: Purple

Imagine being inside your head. It is open, expanded a thousand-fold, and flooded with purple light. As a feeling of peace washes over you, you begin to move forward with astonishing speed.

You sense that you are absorbing everything that passes by you even if you are not conscious of what it is. There is no point at which you end and something else begins. There is no separation. You have merged with the Divine. You are the Universe and the Universe is You.

This is the ultimate feeling of Openness. Not only are you open with your mind and heart, but each cell has expanded to its outer limits. Every molecule of your being is soaking up the gentle lessons that experience offers. Your total receptivity eliminates any obstacles in your life. You navigate easily through every situation.

When you blend with the Universe, you cannot escape its ever present abundance. It will fill your life with prosperity and happiness. Prosperity will become part of you and fill the void where fear and lack previously dwelled.

Openness is a Divine Surrender to Goodness. When you are truly open, you uncover the best in yourself, which is who you really are. Any empty, damaged places within you are magically filled and healed with a Universal medicine that you magnetize to yourself. You become more than you were.

Automatically, you feel a relaxation, a peace of body and soul that you have never experienced before. As you open to the Universe, the worry, fear, and agitation in your life fade and eventually disappear.

You can recreate this sensation anytime you want. Sit quietly and close your eyes. You may wish to hold a piece of Sugilite or our card in your hand, or at our companion chakra, your Third Eye. Imagine an opening between your brows that is filled with our purple light. Move through this opening into your head and observe that the interior is filled with this same color. There are no horizons in any direction. Feel your body gain momentum and begin speeding forward. You have no concerns. You are totally calm and safe.

Notice that your body feels light and spongy. Imagine each cell enlarging time and time again. You feel as though you stretch forever. Your cells allow the Universe's balm to wash through and take up residence inside you. Your body is completely relaxed. You are enveloped in warmth, love, protection, and abundance.

Most people have not experienced this level of receptivity. It is our responsibility and our privilege to describe it to you. Now that you know it is there for you, we urge you to experience the freedom and joy that it allows. With this magnitude of openness, there can be no barriers between you and your Good Fortune. How can you be closed off from something that is part of you?

Through your openness, you create an environment in which you can receive whatever you need. It is not necessary to decide what you should have or what you are worthy of receiving. You can be totally at peace knowing that whatever is for your Highest Good and the Highest Good of the Universe will occur in the right way, in the right time, under the right circumstances. You need not worry or be afraid. You are a child of the Universe, the Generous Provider.

Once you have opened to the Universe, try being more accessible to those closer to home. Extend yourself to your spouse, your animal companion, and the clerk at the store. When others sense that you are open and approachable, they feel relaxed and unintimidated. Your example will inspire them to move closer to the place of openness within themselves.

What issues around openness have drawn you to our card? Would you like to be more open with others? Is there someone that you wish would be more open with you? Would you like to be receptive enough to link with the Divine?

Openness is a gift of enormous value from the Universe. It will change your life. Imagine a world full of completely open beings. What a beautiful world it will be. We are available to help you in any way that we can to reach this place of bliss.

40

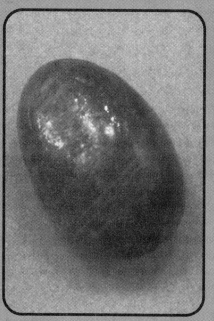

Sunstone

CREATIVITY

Sunstone

CREATIVITY

Chakra: Sacral
Color: Orange

Fire is a magical gift from the Universe. Its warmth and comfort draw you like a magnet. Its flames mesmerize you. As you gaze, transfixed, into the fire, you forge an even greater link to your parent, the Sun— the largest fire you know.

The Sun is the center of creation for your solar system. Without the Sun's energy, Earth would be a dead planet. It provides the spark of light that gently kisses each sleeping entity into wakefulness. Its fiery nature generates the warmth necessary for all growth. Its light psychologically prepares and inspires you for your day's work. Its energy heals your illnesses and diseases.

While the Sun acts as the male aspect, Mother Earth is the receptive womb. She nurtures her children until they are ready to come into the world. She provides a safe haven for their sojourn here. Together, as parents, the Sun and the Earth offer an environment that will nourish their offspring and provide the best chances for survival.

Inside, you have your own sacred fire. This is your gathering place of creativity. This smoldering cauldron, the Sacral or Second chakra, performs a function not unlike that of the uterus in the physical body. It contains the embryos of ideas fueled by Divine Inspiration. It also extends out through your non-physical bodies and unites with the Sun itself—drawing its energy directly from this powerful source of fertility.

Our orange presence is intended to remind you of your alliance with the Sun. Recognizing the Sun's genius for productivity, how can you doubt your own potential? You are here to explore and discover your many talents. And once found, to give them birth.

These abilities were given to you for many reasons: your evolution; your enjoyment and fulfillment; to help yourself and others; to create a healthier, happier world; and to expand the possibilities available in the Universe.

The most conspicuous example of creativity in the Human Kingdom is that of a new baby. What an opportunity to bring into the world a new original with all the possibilities for greatness. One who may be a peacemaker, who may save the environment, or heal the world's diseases. Teach this new being that anything is possible. He or she is not limited in any way. Even those who may appear to have physical, emotional, or mental challenges have unique gifts to offer.

In the Plant Kingdom, new crops and forests continue to burst forth, even against the greatest of odds. Look at the Findhorn Garden, for example. On a frigid, barren, and windy coast of Scotland, a community of determined individuals produced a prolific garden where none had grown before. By communicating with the Nature Spirits, the gardeners learned new ways to grow vegetables and flowers through cooperation with the Plant Kingdom.

In the Mineral Kingdom, even though the time frame seems long by human standards, new islands continue to push up like new sprouts. Volcanoes labor and then give birth to lava from the Earth's core, cleansing and purifying the land nearby.

Avalanches cover soiled ground and uncover new earth so that it may feel the Sun's warm rays.

The Animal Kingdom, like the Human Kingdom, experiences the mystery and beauty of new additions to its population. In every Kingdom, creative events occur that may change the course of history.

Your mind and spirit are fertile ground. They await the seeds of your imagination and ingenuity. Allow them to ripen and mature. Forces all around you are eager to assist in the delivery of your new creation.

Push the edge of the envelope. Attempt something new where you cannot predict the outcome. You may already have an idea that you are hesitant to develop. Go ahead. Take a chance and see what happens.

You like to say, "If you don't use it, you lose it." You never really lose your potential, but you may lose your confidence. Reinforce yourself by venturing into uncharted waters and creating successful experiences.

If you have selected Sunstone as your card today, what is the guidance you seek? Do you want to give birth to the person you would like to become? If so, begin today. You create your world by the way you think, speak, and act. The Universe is not fixed. Your world appears not to change because you believe so firmly that it is permanent and static. Trust us, it can change in the blink of an eye.

Perhaps you desire to pursue a creative interest you have long ignored or a new career path? This is a time of fertility. You are, especially now, able to construct any kind of life for yourself that you can imagine. Sow the seeds. Give birth to your dreams.

A new genesis is in the making. It is inside you. It longs to take its full, first breath. Have courage, sweet friend, your labor will be short and fruitful. Celebrate the birth of a new creation.

41

Tiger's Eye

RIGHT TIMING

Tiger's Eye

RIGHT TIMING

Chakra: Solar Plexus
Color: Gold

When one believes in the concept of right timing, there is no reason for impatience. There is no need for worry. If something is not happening quickly enough for you, do not be concerned. All is as it should be with the timing of that event.

You have heard the expression, "All in good time." The word *good* is a derivation of God. The phrase should more correctly be stated, "All in God's time." Even though from your individual perspective, an event may seem early or late, it always happens at the just the right moment.

The clock and calendar of the Universe are different from those of the physical plane. Whereas your time is fixed and rigid, the timetable of the Universe is variable, dependent on history.

History is not only the Battle of Hastings, JFK's assassination, or your fifteenth birthday. History is also standing in line at the grocery store, sitting in a traffic jam, or waiting for water to boil. History is the passing of time, but also of life incidents, none of which are insignificant.

Life is full of past events. And it will be full of future ones. But more important than either of these, life is full of the present. Most people are not fully conscious in the present. They are preoccupied with what has happened or what will happen.

Be present in the Present. Slow down. Stop thinking about your next appointment. Look around you. Listen to the the hum of voices, machinery, or the absence of it. Feel the texture of the layers of experience all around you. If you had not stopped to notice, you would have missed out on this event in your history.

There may be special moments seeking you out when you are too busy to notice. Good Fortune may be looking for an opening to share itself with you. If you are speeding impatiently toward your future, you will not be able to make the connection with your possible destinies. Life will stream by you, an endless succession of meetings, activities, and other obligations.

Whatever you are doing, wherever you are, immerse yourself in the experience. If you feel impatient, you are thinking more about where you are going to be than where you are. Patience is fueled by the faith that all will happen as it should and when it should. If you forced to wait in a long grocery line, perhaps it is because you are supposed to encounter an old friend in the parking lot. Your schedule and hers have to coincide perfectly for the meeting to occur.

Right timing is not the perceived best timing for one individual. It is the best timing for an intricately woven web of millions of entities all affecting each other. The Universe orchestrates the circumstances and timing that will impact the greatest number for the Highest Good.

What timing issues caused you to draw our card today? If something you want to happen in your life seems unduly delayed, consider why it has not occurred yet. Is it for the Highest Good of all who are involved? Does everyone benefit as a result of what will happen? Can you relinquish your own timetable in favor of right timing, whenever that may be?

Ask for guidance as to the reason for the delay. Then let it go. Insistence can make matters worse. You may effectively create a situation that you insist upon, only to later wish you had not.

Our golden color and energy correspond perfectly to that of the Solar Plexus chakra which we assist. The Solar Plexus is the center of personal power in the Self. One aspect of power is knowing when to use your will and when not to. Always move positively forward, but let the Universe take care of timing.

You have heard that there are no mistakes or coincidences. We also tell you that things do not happen at the wrong time. The Universe runs on right timing. Likewise, so do you. You are a timepiece ticking at your own pace. Your rhythm is your vibration or frequency.

Do you worry that your spiritual development is slower than you would like? You are evolving in perfect timing. You can never measure your progress against another person's. Each of you is working on an entirely different timetable. It is necessary that you work through your own unique series of experiences before certain key, life-changing events will occur. Time spent agonizing over your lack of progress only erects roadblocks in your path.

Allow the Universal Timekeeper to work its magic. Patience and positive effort draw the abundance of the Universe to you. A calm, trusting spirit will allow you to recognize and welcome serendipity when it arrives. Set aside your worry. Everything is occurring at the right time. Make the most of it.

42

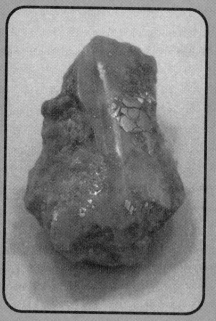

Turquoise

Faith

Turquoise

FAITH

Chakra: Thymus
Color: Blue-Green

In your modern world, most of you are able to meet your survival needs by purchasing clothes, food, and shelter. Even those who are homeless and destitute persevere by their own ingenuity and determination. The will to survive is deeply implanted within each of you.

What concerns us is your will to *live*. Many of you have lost faith that you have a chance for happiness. You doubt that the world is a kind, nurturing place. You no longer believe that you can make a difference.

In ancient times, people were driven toward survival as well. They required tenacity of spirit to hang on under the most difficult and dangerous of conditions. They had to build their houses, grow their food, make their clothes, protect themselves from severe weather and ferocious animals. Faith in their purpose helped them survive.

At first, they persisted on a day-to-day physical level, building villages, then towns and cities. Once established, they felt a consuming desire to expand, learn, and live. They had faith that they could build a better world. These ancients were planting roots for all of you who followed. Not only did they build huts and palaces with mortar and bricks, they constructed societies with ideas and beliefs.

You have an opportunity today to do what the ancients did so

301

long ago. To create a new world. There is a need today, greater than in olden times, to fuse a new culture, one built on hope and faith. You can be a ground breaker for a new way of thinking. This is its basis: the Universe supports you and cares about you. You have countless unseen friends helping you through each of your challenges. You are never alone.

It is within your power, through faith, to create a beautiful, joy-filled existence for yourself. Peace can become a reality in your world. "What about all the wars and hatred?" you ask. It is true, that is one reality out there and some people will choose to live in it.

But there are many possible realities co-existing. You can live in one of happiness, love, peace, and prosperity. How? By choosing to. Your faith that it can happen—and your words and behavior confirming this reality—construct a real, tangible environment. It can be as substantial as the structures built by ancient masons.

It may sound naive and simplistic to say that "Faith can move mountains." But this is the truth that you have forgotten. Negativity and pessimism have killed it inside you.

Talk to people who have created a beautiful, well-balanced life for themselves. We feel sure that they used their imaginations, envisioned a dream, and had faith that their dreams could come true.

They allowed their faith to overcome their doubt. They intended a direction that they wanted to move in long before a specific goal had taken form. Conviction and determination helped them achieve their success.

Faith is driven by persistence. Persistence is fed by determination. Determination is nurtured by investing one's time, emotions, physical labor, and spirit into a project.

If obstacles appear in your way, go around them. These roadblocks are simply testing your commitment. Although they may appear insurmountable, they are only an inconvenience and will crumble when your intention is spoken clearly from your heart. Humans have a resilient spirit. Bounce back and set out on a new course.

Why have you have drawn our card today? Are you doubting that circumstances will turn out the way you have planned? Have you lost faith in yourself, a relationship, or society itself? What will restore your faith?

Life is more than physical survival. Life is ecstasy. It is possible to have Heaven on Earth. Try adopting a new perspective for a few days. Assume that life can be blissful. Give in to optimism. See how different you feel. When others notice a difference in you, tell them what has happened. They may have been waiting for a glimmer of hope in their life. You may be their inspiration.

In ancient times, indigenous peoples of several continents regarded us as a symbol of faith. Today, we are honored to again communicate and reinforce this concept to the Human Kingdom.

At one time, Turquoise was associated with the Throat chakra. Now we are one of many stones who is moving to assist the emerging chakra between Heart and Throat, the Thymus chakra. We are helping the Thymus chakra complete itself with an infusion of our blue-green energy.

This new chakra is materializing now as a response to the worldwide reclaiming of self that is occurring. The Thymus chakra is involved with an expression of self that cannot occur until the lost parts of one's life puzzle have been found and put in their proper place. Faith is a critical component of this equation. Have faith in yourself and in the happier, healthier life you can build. Faith will take you as far as you need to go.

If you have lost your faith, you can regain it by remembering a different world that once existed. A world of hope, joy, and love. Its memory lies deep inside you. Trust that life can be different. Let this feeling blossom again in you. Let your faith be an example for all the world to see.

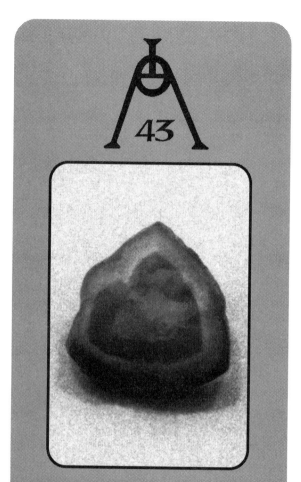

Watermelon
Tourmaline

Unconditional Love

Watermelon Tourmaline

UNCONDITIONAL LOVE

Chakra: Heart
Color: Green and Pink

The first step to unconditional love is loving yourself unconditionally. In the Universal School of Love, self-love must precede love of others for a very practical reason. Love of self is the beginning, a kindergarten for testing out the love experience. It is a space to explore new feelings and experiences. You discover and play with them, paint them into your life, and mold them into expression. They are your teachers.

Self-love is important practice for opening your heart to others. If you can forgive yourself for your perceived misdeeds and imperfections, you will be capable of doing the same for others. You must release self-blame before you can truly embrace all other creatures.

You have grown accustomed to giving love based on deservedness—when someone has been kind to you or when you consider them to be a good person. What about people who have hurt you or appear to be despicable in some way? Are they less deserving of love? In reality, they may need a lot more love than the folks who seem more worthy.

Unconditional Love means that there are no strings attached—no conditions placed on your gift of love. The Universe makes no distinction about the worthiness of recipients for love and abundance. In its eyes, all are created from the Original Spark, and, therefore, all are filled with Divine Light.

Do you always give altruistically? There may be times when you give of yourself because you feel obligated, guilty, or pressured from external forces. Do not chastise yourself for what you might consider to be unpure motives. See those incidents for what they are, but understand that this is not the same as unconditional love. When giving comes from a place of unconditional love, fellowship is shared between two souls and hearts are opened.

The melding of the pink and green energies of our colors represent the reverence of self and the reverence of others, part of the domain of the Heart chakra. Our physical structure shows how the two travel together as interlocking complimentary aspects of each other. They are the Yin and the Yang of love expression, the inturning and the outpouring of love.

Unkind, hurtful behavior is a distortion of Universal Goodness and Godliness. But the soul learns through experiences. In the process, it may get banged around and lash out with negativity. This may be undesirable and repugnant. However, it is part of the process of duality that must be experienced before the natural returning to The Light.

The return to Wholeness is a reabsorption of dark into light. It is a decision that must be consciously entered into by each individual. To provide the soul with the necessary information for growth, you must experiment with both the light and dark expressions of your character throughout many incarnations. After numerous adventures testing each side out, you will decide which path you want to follow.

You have selected our card because unconditional love wants to express itself in your life. You may be the giver or the receiver. Regardless, you will learn more about unconditional love through your experience with it. What do you need to understand about unconditional love that will allow you to express or receive it more fully? Do you feel that you are loving unconditionally? If not, how can you bring this energy into your life? What steps can you take?

Although it appears to be a contradiction, unconditional love, ironically, has some conditions that it places on you. One prerequisite for unconditional love is allowing others to be who they are and not who you want them to be. As long as they must meet some pre-specified goal of yours, they will likely fall short and appear unworthy of your love. They are worthy because they exist—not because they meet standards that you or others set for them.

Judgmental criteria are human constructs that have no relationship to Universal Truth. Prejudices are illusions that humans create to separate and elevate themselves. If you compare yourself with a serial killer, you will feel self-righteous that you are a better person. That is, until you realize that you may have taken on a similar dark role for self-expression in another lifetime. Consequently, the release of judgment is essential in opening the heart in unconditional love.

Forgiveness is also a fundamental component of unconditional love. If you are harboring resentment toward others, it will be impossible to truly love them. Try to see their abusive or neglectful behavior as the tormented acting-out of people in great agony. Although it may not appear so on the surface, we can assure you their souls are under siege. They have lost their true selves and are flailing away in the wilderness to find them. Unfortunately, in the process, you may be subjected to their insensitivity or cruelty.

Let the pain, anger, and bitterness surface in your heart. Grieve for yourself and the others involved. Purge your soul of this darkness that has possessed you for such a long time. It has imprisoned you. Set yourself and the perpetrators free.

Look around you in your life and see the opportunities for unconditional love. Love yourself, a parent, a sibling, a boss, a friend, the alcoholic on the corner, the rapist, the murderer. Giving love to some people may be easier than others, at first. Remember that the kindergarten foundation is necessary for the graduating diploma.

Unconditional love is purely motivated by compassion, caring, and an open heart. The bonus is that love given with the intention of helping, healing, and allowing returns the same experience to the giver. Although never the intention of unconditional love, it is a delightful unexpected benefit. Above all, do not forget that you are profoundly deserving of the same unconditional love that you extend to others.

44

Zincite

SENSUALITY

Zincite

SENSUALITY

Chakra: Sacral
Color: Deep Orange-Red and Light Orange

Sensuality can be a physical, emotional, or spiritual experience. A bite of your favorite chocolate pie. A beautiful voice singing. The ocean's warm waves lapping at your legs. Your cat's purr. Walking barefoot on cool grass. Sipping a lemonade. The texture of velvet. A massage. The smell of popcorn. Holding hands. Union with the Divine.

One of the most delightful ways to explore the realm of sensuality is through sex. However, sex appears to be a troublesome area. Many humans are confused about whether sexual pleasure is good or bad. Society's messages are mixed on this issue too.

Movies, TV, books, and music are filled with sexual erotica. Sexual exploitation sells toothpaste, cars, and computers. Humans learn more about the dance of sensuality from the media than from their own instincts. By all appearances, your world seems very sexually oriented.

And yet, many of your religious institutions teach that sex is an act of functionality—intended primarily to populate the planet with more *like minded* humans, thereby, perpetuating particular belief systems. They neglect to discuss or endorse its pleasurable sensations. In many cultures, you have been taught that when you give in to your sexual instincts, you revert to degenerate behavior. Sensuality implies a loss of control and, therefore, must be *bad*.

313

Many of you who are well-adjusted and sexually active may still have some unconscious hang-ups about sex. Is feeling pleasure hedonistic, immoral, and depraved? Or is it blissful, ecstatic, and sacred? Some of your past programming affects your enjoyment of sex.

Regardless of what anyone tells you, the major purpose of sex is not to make babies. Sex was designed to give you pleasure. If all the Great Creator wanted was for humans to procreate, the most boring, clinical methods would have worked just as well.

Instead, sexual pleasure is intended as an explosion of the senses. It blends anticipation, excitement, and euphoria with intimacy. Sexual fulfillment is a Divine gift. It replicates, on the physical plane, the joy of ultimate union with the Universe. It is the feeling of losing yourself and finding yourself, both at the same moment. Sensuality is designed to create a greater sense of self-awareness.

Unfortunately, some of you have had negative experiences with sex, making the accompanying physical pleasure seem obscene. If you felt pleasure in those instances, you are not a bad person. Your body's response and the psychological or emotional trauma you endured operate separately. You were sensing the natural instrumentation of your body. It is programmed to elicit pleasurable feelings during sexual activity.

Or your problem may be just the opposite. Perhaps you have linked your current sexual activity with past unpleasant incidents. If so, you may not be experiencing pleasure at all. Look at your present situation and determine whether it works for your Highest Good or not. If it is does not, get out of it.

If it does, recognize that the past experience and the present one are not the same. Appreciate the new one for what it is and, if possible, try to let go of the other. If you need more clarity or support, seek professional help. Remember that you celebrate your life and yourself when you feel pleasure.

If you have drawn this card, take a look at how much sensuality and pleasure you are allowing into your life. Pleasure is part of the joy of life waiting to share itself with you.

It is the nature of the Senses to operate sensually. If you cut yourself off from sensuality, you miss out on so much of the human experience. Why have these senses if you only experience them at such a small percentage of their power?

We are the color of deep orange-red with encrustations of light orange. We work with the Sacral or Second chakra, the center of pleasure, sexuality, sensuality, creativity, and reproduction. Is one or more of these dynamics calling to you for more attention? Or conversely, if you are overly focused in an area, it may require less.

The law of the Universe is balance. Balance is the ideal state. Each of the chakras oversees an area of human potential. Each is subject to excess or deprivation. If each area gets exercised equally, your life will be balanced.

So many non-physical beings yearn for your corporeal existence. To sense—to feel—is a special privilege. Do not deny the lifeforce within you. Enjoy this great gift. We rejoice in your sensuality and your humanity.

Remember . . .

...Believe In Yourself